*Captive Continent*

# Captive Continent

The Stockholm Syndrome in European-Soviet Relations

PHILIP PILEVSKY

New York
Westport, Connecticut
London

**Library of Congress Cataloging-in-Publication Data**

Pilevsky, Philip.
  Captive continent : the Stockholm syndrome in European-Soviet
relations / Philip Pilevsky.
    p. cm.
  Bibliography: p.
  Includes index.
  ISBN 0-275-93064-5 (alk. paper)
  1. Europe—Foreign relations—Soviet Union—Psychological aspects.
2. Soviet Union—Foreign relations—Europe—Psychological aspects.
3. Europe—Foreign relations—1945-  —Psychological aspects.
I. Title.
D1065.S65P53  1989
327.4047—dc19            88-26573

Library of Congress Catalog Card Number: 88-26573
ISBN: 0-275-93064-5

First published in 1989

Praeger Publishers, One Madison Avenue, New York, NY 10010
A division of Greenwood Press, Inc.

Printed in the United States of America

The paper used in this book complies with the
Permanent Paper Standard issued by the National
Information Standards Organization (Z39.48-1984).

10 9 8 7 6 5 4 3 2 1

*This book is dedicated in memory of*
*Chaim Pilevsky and Jack Peerless*

# Contents

# *Acknowledgments*

I would like to express my thanks to all who have helped me in one way or another to write this book: to my wife Reneé for making everything I do possible; to Lynette Luyt for her sustained interest and useful suggestions; to Elaine Gallis, Eileen Kircher, Rose Marie Melendez, and Thelma Bowdler, who assisted in the execution of the text and general editing.

I am especially indebted to Kenneth Shouler for enthusiasm and belief in the book as well as judicious improvements in the writing and analysis.

# Introduction

ιn a *New York Times* magazine article dated April 7, 1986, a prominent world leader was quoted as saying, "The Soviet Union's struggle for detente is genuine. Even if Moscow sometimes has an active presence outside its borders! This presence—in such places as Afghanistan, Hungary and Czechoslovakia—was the result of its efforts to guard against United States expansionism."[1]

It is obvious that this statement betrays significant sympathies toward the Soviet Union. In the statement the speaker has accused the United States of expansionism and has apparently excused all Soviet influence beyond its borders. How is it possible to use this kind of special pleading? How is it that the speaker could (1) interpret U.S. interest in the world as expansionism and (2) believe that the Soviet actions do not constitute expansionism? As is common with double-standard arguments, one standard is reserved for a special acquaintance, while a quite different one is used for "others."

Before the reader makes the assumption that the speaker is a member of the Soviet politburo or a member of a Communist party, let me introduce him. He is a very influential head of state: Greek Prime Minister Andreas Papandreous.

What is the significance of such a statement by a Western leader? The answer lies in the reader's willingness to examine the current political atmosphere in Europe in a new and different way.

Something is happening in the political atmosphere in Europe. It is evident in such seemingly inconsequential actions as a change in Sweden's official second language from French to Russian, to matters of greater consequence, such as the reluctance on the part of some European governments to contribute their fair share to the North Atlantic Treaty Organization's (NATO's) defense structure.

It is also evident in a European peace movement, a movement that grew up in those very countries where old U.S. missiles were replaced by newer Pershings and cruise missiles and at a time when Reagan's military buildup threatened to upset the Soviet's position of military superiority. Since this installation of new missiles, the World Peace Council finds a greater threat of nuclear war.

This viewpoint suggests that fear has entered the realm of European politics. But fear can be a numbing and irrational force. So irrational as to lead some people to await the abolition of the police because the criminals are becoming too aggressive. A psychoanalyst might construe this behavior as the replacement of a real object of fear with an imaginary one.

To those willing to look closely, there has been a definite shift in European sympathies. This shift has taken the form of either "nationalistic" neutralism or a pro-Soviet position on many significant issues.

We have seen Europe reluctant to respond in harmony to U.S. calls for strong and cohesive action against international threats, such as terrorism and Soviet-backed aggression. The European community has turned away from U.S. requests for sanctions against the Soviet Union or its satellites, even where there has been clear evidence of a Soviet connection to international atrocities.

Recent evidence for this conclusion abounds. To begin with, the meltdown at the Chernobyl plant was not singled out for disapproval by Europe's antinuclear and disarmament groups. One activist claimed that he took part in demonstrations against the United States after the Libyan raid but would not protest at the Soviet embassy in London. "This (accident) isn't an example of Russian aggression. It could happen anywhere."[2] If the pronoun "it" signifies the entire incident, coverup included, then his statement is extremely doubtful. And extremely accommodating.

Nor were anti-Libyan sanctions carried out by our allies, despite a strong antiterrorist statement composed by the leaders of seven industrial democracies. Across Europe the Libyan raid was denounced as an instance of unwarranted aggression, frightfully similar to Gorbachev's view that it was "barbarous."

Still more recently, the decision in Washington to discontinue the SALT (Strategic Arms Limitations Talks) II treaty has produced great clamoring in the alliance. Regardless of the treaty's flaws and obsolete conditions and the Soviet's indulgent disregard for its specifications, European leaders, like the Soviets, perceived the decision in Washington as intending to finish any manner of arms control. This conclusion simply doesn't follow from the decision.

It is not enough to presume that the strains in the relationships between Europe and the United States are simply political or economic. It is not enough to suggest that they will correct themselves. Nor is it enough to conclude that meetings, summits, or careful policies will improve matters.

The European–U.S. "family" has been disrupted. The Soviets have been engaged in a long-term strategy to bring about that disruption. The Soviets would welcome our disappearance from the NATO sphere of influence.

The Soviets' intentions, Europe's reaction, and the United States' apparent inability to influence the shift in balance all transcend the political and the economic. What we are witnessing is a profound psychological dynamic in effect. We see Europe shifting from its identification with the United States in favor of an identification with the Soviet Union. A British independent television poll indicated that the majority of participants believe that Britain's relationship with the United States is "harmful." Only 39 percent said it was "helpful."[3]

A new and profound bond is being formed. The bond seems to be secured by Europe's own fear and dependence. Understanding this bond and the dynamics of its formation will help answer the questions that arise concerning Europe's shifting allegiance. The bond and its consequent relationship is most clearly characterized by the Stockholm Syndrome.

Essential to the Stockholm Syndrome is the identification by captives or hostages with their captors. The *Longman Dictionary of Psychology and Psychiatry* explains identification with the aggressor as "an unconscious mechanism in which the individual identifies with an opponent he cannot master. This occasionally occurred in concentration camps, and according to psychoanalysts, occurs on a developmental level when the male child identifies with his rival, the Father, toward the end of the Oedipal phase." But identification can also occur with any person, group, object, nation, or deity on whom someone may be dependent. Hostages and nations are prime candidates for displaying the dependence that would lead them to identify with some "provider." We explore this psychological dynamic at length in Chapter 4.

Volumes have been written studying the effects on individuals who have been kidnapped or taken hostage. Dozens of contemporary examples, little known and discussed, substantiate this behavior pattern of identification. We will examine some of these cases in Chapters 1 and 2. The modern body of research dates back to observations of the behavior of inmates in the Nazi concentration camps and continues on to such terrorist incidents as the capturing of the *Achille Lauro* and the hijacking of the TWA 847 in June of 1985.

The contribution this book makes to the discussion of U.S.–European policy and the influence of the Soviet Union on the psyche of Europe is to interpret current events and trends in light of psychological insight and the Stockholm Syndrome. This book will argue that Europe, in the most profoundly psychological way, is being held hostage by the Soviet Union. Evidence in the form of recent events substantiates this conclusion.

I do not employ the term "hostage" without sober regard to the significance of my accusation. Psychological research firmly establishes the principle that hostages will, given a certain set of conditions, identify with their captors against the police. Victims of hostage syndrome, or the Stockholm Syndrome, will identify the police or other authorities as the enemy.

The label "Stockholm Syndrome" was coined due to the behavior of four bank employees who were captives in the vault of a Stockholm bank. One of the captives recalled, "We weren't with the police. We imagined we could protect ourselves from them. We believed in Jan [Olsson, the captor]."[4] Four years later, a Hanafi Muslim attack on the B'nai B'rith building in Washington, D.C., ended with the same result: The captives berated the police after the event and had frequent praise for their captors.

Terrified persons, including captives in Europe, know in their heart of hearts who the real source of danger is. But side by side with this knowledge resides fear, a fear that anything angering the Soviets is dangerous for that reason.

Andreas Papandreous's statement suggests a chillingly similar idea. He defends Soviet expansion, even to the point of naming the countries where it has most violently occurred, while at the same moment pointing a finger toward the United States and accusing it, like a hostage would of the police, of the real crime. Shortly after the Reykjavik summit polls taken traced a sharp decline in U.S. popular standing. Forty-three percent of West Germans blamed Reagan for the failure of the Reykjavik summit, and only 6 percent blamed Gorbachev.

Only in France among the major European NATO states was opinion more evenly divided.[5]

Our discussion of the Stockholm Syndrome and its relevance to Europe must take us along two parallel roads. Along the first, we must clearly delineate the syndrome and determine its bearing on Europe. The second road must also show clearly the Soviet's participation in a strategy to make Europe hostage.

For Europe, much of its shift in identification is unconscious, just as a child's identification is unconscious. Survival situations bring this unconscious mechanism into clear light. Identification with the aggressor deals with the deepest layers of one's person, stirring unconscious memories of one's earliest patterns of dependence and order. Not only did this response occur in prisoners of war in Korea and Indo-China, but in Auschwitz too. Inmates in Auschwitz, in order to survive, tried to behave like their captors. Had they not done so, they might have been overwhelmed by fears of death, chaos, and the elimination of all norms.

"To really feel in such a situation is a risk," argued Yale psychologist Robert Lifton. In a hostage environment a process called "psychic numbing" is developed, explained Lifton, in order to protect the agent from feeling.[6] This kind of defense against feeling can successfully enable a captive to identify with some provider. Reviewing the Stockholm case, Nils Bejerot stated, "It is to be expected that after a point a bond of friendship springs up between victims and their captors."[7]

For the parent, and for the captor, there can be, and usually is, consciousness. Banks are not robbed by accident, nor are terrorist accidents brought about by chance. Both kinds of crimes are planned carefully. So, too, has the Soviet Union defined its strategy.

The Soviet Union has long been aware of the hostage–captor relationship. The Soviets have actively sought, in word and deed, to impose on Europe the psychological criteria that would make it hostage. Like a captor, they create unending stress, usually effected by their military negotiating and movements. But sometimes they reflect the captor in another guise: They dress up their most threatening deeds with a human face. In May 1986 we witnessed Gorbachev gushing over with concern for Western Europe, trying to effect a ban on nuclear testing, not two weeks after the coverup at Chernobyl.

Like a captor carrying out a mission, he tries to provide evidence for a "human disposition," if only to bury our memory of an event that reflected no humanity in the first place. "But just imagine that it was discovered that there was American uranium that burned up in Chernobyl," mused Karl Fedmeyer, a commentator for the *Frankfurter Allgemeine Zeitung* in West Germany. "Then we would have plenty of anti-Reagan demonstrations. This is the state of opinion in this country."[8] And this state of opinion has been advantageous to the Soviet cause.

In the course of the past twenty years, the Soviets have engaged in a strategy that has eroded the U.S. military advantage over the Soviet Union. This strategy has sown dissension among the United States' European allies. While building their own arsenal, the Soviets have confused the Europeans into thinking their security lies in disarmament. This strategy is continued by Gorbachev. During 1986, Gorbachev became increasingly vocal in his advocacy of the concept of "Europe for the Europeans." Not only did he call for reductions in Soviet and U.S. troops in Europe, but he expressed the view that military alliances like NATO and the Warsaw Pact were obsolete and ought to be disbanded.[9]

During the past twenty years, the most dramatically since the 1970s, the United States has engaged in a downward arms control spiral that has contributed greatly to the loss of its worldwide superiority. If this spiral were allowed to continue, the United States would find itself locked permanently into the position of a second-rate military power. Détente (a French word for "relaxation"), although it "eased tensions" between the United States and the Soviets, caused the Americans to lose vast ground in the arms race. Now the United States has accommodated Gorbachev in his desire to rid Europe of its nuclear deterrent.

The position of this book is not anti-Soviet. Rather, it is to alarm policy makers to the psychological realities that affect the European decisions regarding current events. The position of this book is that the United States must continue any and all negotiations with the Soviet Union, from arms control to cultural exchanges. But the United States must negotiate from strength. Part of this strength must come from a deep understanding of the Soviet Union's methods and goals, as well as the effectiveness of those methods on the Europeans. One of the crucial perceptions of the Reagan administration is that negotiation with the Soviets is only fruitful when it's done from a position of strength; hence the initial arms buildup in the early 1980s in order to bring the Soviets to the table.

An example of the kind of strength needed is found in Washington's decision to scrap SALT II. Why is this kind of strength needed?

Evidence from SALT I, SALT II, and START (Strategic Arms Reduction Talks) negotiations suggests that the Soviet Union first decides what arms it requires to meet its strategic objectives and then concentrates on constraining, by negotiations, the United States' ability to counter those objectives.

The story about missiles is a long and unfinished one. But suffice it to say that we do not know what we ought to about the Soviet Union's military strength, because we cannot know by our present means of verification (namely, satellites and electronic intelligence). But it is safe to say that a condition of strategic parity exists between the superpowers.

The primary goal of Soviet world hegemony has never been a secret. But its methods and specific strategies, especially those concerned with Europe, seem to have too often eluded U.S. policy makers. Part of the purpose of this book is to elucidate those strategies so that the West can better cope with its ability to form a Soviet foreign policy.

This book suggests that for the first time it is necessary to conjoin two basic concepts in a unique way; conjoin the communist goal of hegemony and the reality of the hostage syndrome.

It is the very nature of the Soviet system not to rest contented until this goal of hegemony is achieved. The Soviets employ the same strategies in dealing with Europe that captors use to hold their captives. But they further resemble captors in their purposive behavior; they employ congenial actions as political means to a greater political end.

The Soviets long ago understood the value of strength and the appearance of strength in implementing their strategies. Just as an authoritarian parent will impose its will on a child, so too does the Soviet Union try to impose its will on Europe. I am not suggesting that Europe is a child, but dependence is an aspect of a child's behavior, and Europe is drifting toward a greater dependence on the Soviet Union. Chapter 5 addresses Soviet–Western European relations from the standpoint of Soviet objectives.

Over the course of the past twenty years, the Soviet Union has initiated and the United States and Europe have participated in the policy of détente. For the many positive things that one could say about détente, there are an equal number of negatives. But the most disturbing negative is that détente has given the Soviets their most effective tool for influencing Europe. It has given the Soviet Union the tool to make Europe a hostage.

For many years, talks between the East and West have been more "face-saving" exercises for the governments involved than they have been exercises in diplomacy. The "face-saving" qualities of these talks have intensified in recent years. When Yuri Andropov assumed control of the Soviet state after the death of Leonid Brezhnev, negotiations between the governments of the Soviet Union and the United States had become, in the words of Strobe Talbott in his book *The Russians and Reagan*, full-dress presidential speech making: "The result was a game of high-level, high-visibility, high-volume one-upmanship that made progress behind closed doors all the more difficult."[10] Recent occurrences, far from disproving this thesis, have all but confirmed it. Whenever an event of international significance occurs—like Libya, Chernobyl, or the controversy over SALT II—an extended rally of verbal missiles flies.

Talbott referred to this process as the "opposite of summitry." Why does this process continue to occur? There are many possible answers, but the one that seems to make the most sense from Andropov's point of view is relatively simple. Andropov did not want to engage in a serious dialogue with the United States if the goal of such a dialogue was to bring about military parity between the two superpowers and relief from the threat of nuclear war. Without this threat the Soviet Union would lack one of the tools necessary to make Western Europe its own, namely the ability to effect fear and stress with nuclear weapons.

Andropov was instead taking his cues from his predecessors. He was continuing a public relations stance that had in mind one audience—Western Europe.

The goal of the Soviet public relations campaign has always been used to create the impression, the myth, that it is they who are the peacemakers. According to that message, it is the Americans who constantly seek war.

A speech by Andrei Gromyko, the Soviet minister of foreign affairs, on the foreign policy of the Soviet Union illustrates this tendency: "Everything in the name of man, everything for the good of man, manifests itself in the aims pursued by our foreign policy. They are, first of all, the elimination of danger and the consolidation of peace." Later in the speech he alleged: "The United States of America has continuously, year after year, tried to increase the scale of the production of arms, especially those of mass annihilation."[11] And Soviet propagandists have always emphasized the contrast between "peace-loving Europeans" and the transatlantic "warmongers."

Gorbachev enjoys using this message to sow divisions in the Atlantic alliance. The alliance is presently split over what to do about NATO's remaining nuclear forces, and Gorbachev can be expected to prey on these differences, emphasizing the basic principles of his foreign policy—"peace, peaceful coexistence, equality and mutually beneficial cooperation." Meanwhile, the Soviets continue to modernize their forces.[12]

The former representative of the Mutual and Balanced Force Reduction talks (MBFR) has claimed "to believe that Gorbachev will rescue the West from its conventional inferiority is to be on the lookout for Santa."[13]

The serious student of Soviet affairs would do well to notice that as they claim the title of peacemaker, the Soviets are also maneuvering their armies and weapons to heighten the atmosphere of fear and tension plaguing the world and most particularly in Western Europe. The percentage of their gross national product (GNP) spent on military exceeds that of any NATO nation and the United States.

Returning to the Greek Prime Minister Papandreous, it is apparent that the Soviet propaganda has been successful. He has accorded them the position of peacemaker while accusing the United States of expansionism. Even a conservative member of the British Parliament, Cyril Townsend—not to mention the Labor leader Neil Kinnock—attacked the United States' decision to scrap SALT II, while maintaining in the next breath, "Of course I fully agree that there have been Soviet violations."

And this is not all. The Soviet-controlled World Peace Council spreads the message that as soon as the West disarms itself, the Soviets will follow suit, and with incredible gullibility they urge us to "try" this suicidal experiment. The only movement that did not condemn the Soviets' invasion of Afghanistan was this movement.

The British Council for Nuclear Development (CND) acts in kind. This movement put out a booklet entitled, "Program for Action" in which Americans are depicted as warlike because of their stock of missiles. But the booklet contains not a single mention of the hundreds of Soviet SS-20s already aimed at Europe. This nuclear fright message has even convinced certain church groups in the competition for public opinion in Europe.

Across the continent of Europe there are massive gatherings protesting the installation of U.S. missiles. Evidence reveals that the peace movements are Soviet sponsored—that the Soviets lay out more than $50 million a year to organize protesters and even reward the organizers with all-expenses-paid trips to Soviet resorts.[14] The only purpose of the U.S. missiles is to offset the threat of the Soviet missiles already stationed in Eastern Europe.

Millions of persons in Great Britain, Belgium, Holland, France, Italy, and Germany are marching about, claiming that the threat of war comes from their own government and the government of the United States. It is not only the young and college students who participate in these protests. We hear among the voices members of European governments.

There are often other indications that Europe's identification has shifted away from the United States toward the East. Europe has agreed to go ahead and assist the Soviets with their gas pipeline in spite of U.S. pleas for boycott. After the hijacking of the luxury liner *Achille Lauro*, the Italian prime minister protested *against* the United States' action of intercepting an Egyptian airliner in order to bring to trial the terrorists who murdered a U.S. citizen. In fact, Craxi resigned his post because of the incident. And the *Achille Lauro* was an Italian ship.

European governments were unanimous in resisting calls for sanctions against Libya in the wake of recent terrorist attacks in airports at Vienna and Rome. Intelligence sources have determined that Libya has been instrumental in the training and supplying of international terrorism.

This increased endeavor not to give offense to the Soviets in Western Europe has even more recent illustrations. Despite signing a "tough" antiterrorist statement in May 1986, seven heads of industrial democracies came out against using force in Libya. Across the continent Americans were being accused of "Rambomania." Both the United States, and Margaret Thatcher for supporting Reagan, were assailed by the British press. One headline, THATCHER GETS HER COMEUPPANCE, appearing in the *Manchester Guardian Weekly*, celebrated Thatcher's loss of popularity in Parliament because of her pro-Reagan stance. Another headline boomed, THATCHER SURRENDERS TO REAGAN'S GUNBOAT POLICY.[15] Because she supported U.S. policies, Thatcher was found guilty by association.

What logic can one find in the European reaction to these events? Basically, one must suggest that the governments of Europe are acting and reacting like persons totally hostage to the Soviets. What else can one conclude when logic and clear thinking are conspicuously absent from their viewpoints and actions?

There are several conditions that must exist for the Stockholm Syndrome to take effect. First and foremost, there needs to be an extremely high level of stress. This stress effectively forces a psychological regression on the part the victims to a more childlike time. Among other things, this state is characterized by dependence, which has its own psychological dynamic and often leads an individual to identify with a father, a deity, or some other kind of authority.

The Soviet Union has created and maintains that stress every day with its global posturing. The focal point of that stress has been Western Europe. This stress is heightened by their recent attempts at negotiating the removal of U.S. arms from European soil.

Second, the Stockholm Syndrome requires a certain length of time for the bond of identification to develop and take hold. This length of time is also dependent on the extent of the stress in the situation. For the application of the Stockholm Syndrome on the continent of Europe, we would expect the necessary time to be greatly exaggerated.

As previously mentioned, Khrushchev began the public relations message and method that continued through the mid-1950s, at the height of the cold war era. What this means is that détente and its underlying framework have been the core of Soviet policy for about thirty years. The importance of détente, as a foreign policy serving Soviet ends, is discussed in Chapter 6.

A third criterion for the Stockholm Syndrome is that hostages must perceive their captors in a "positive" light. Thirty years of hearing the myth of the Soviet Union as a peacemaker has created in Europeans of this generation a real confusion as to who does represent peace in this world, the Soviet Union or the United States. As we shall see, to hostages, positive really means the absence of negative, nothing more.

The importance of this positive perception, which I will fully develop later, can be seen in a brief example of Barry Rosen, an American captive in Iran. When he was about to be released, the guard spoke in Farsi (an Iranian dialect): "You and several others have been selected for possible release. I just want to remind you how humane our treatment has been—so if you get out, you'll tell the truth."[16] Rosen grew incensed and lost control, berating the Iranians for treating him like an animal. He expressed hate for their ideology and country and said he would never forgive them. In this instance there was no positive perception of the captor, and so an important requirement for Stockholm Syndrome was lacking. Had Rosen perceived his captors in a favorable way, a bond of identification would have prevented his harsh rebuke of the prison guard. He later recalled, "I just would not beg."

But fundamental to the Stockholm Syndrome is again the notion of stress born of factors like uncertainty, material deprivation, physical and psychological discomfort, and so on. Captors must create in their hostages an almost Machiavellian fear—fear of pain or even death. They must maintain the highest level of stress and tension possible, relieving it only to create a greater dependency on them by the hostages.

A fear of this magnitude has become a given in everyday life in Europe. One can see it in the faces of Europeans. Walking the streets of Europe, the only smiling faces one will encounter is of Americans visiting. As one commentator remarked, ''What one sees is not so much a case of objective impotence as of a debilitating self-perception: We are weak, we are dependent, we cannot afford heroic gestures.''[17]

Europe is a continent in fear. This fear is as concrete as the wall dividing East from West Berlin. It is as immediate as the few seconds it would take for any of the missiles lining the Warsaw Pact countries to arrive in any European capital.

In describing how fear can produce a ''survival mentality,'' Christopher Lasch wrote: ''The experience of survivalism . . . can destroy the capacity for resistance by destroying the sense of personal responsibility.'' As a victim, real or imaginary, ''One finally learns to confront life not as a moral agent, but solely as a passive victim, and political protest degenerates into a whine of self-pity.''[18]

The experience of mass death in European wars and the possibility of annihilation has engendered a survival ethic in Europe. And just as a hostage's attempt to survive is not blameworthy, a nation's desire to survive, pure and simple, is not wholly blameworthy. But it is appropriate to condemn those advocates of nuclear disarmament and other persons who can conceive of no higher object than mere survival, even if it means surrendering their knowledge and rationality in exchange for national security.

This kind of fear that grows from a survival ethic is greatly escalated by scientific and technological achievements. Elizabeth Kubler-Ross, a medical doctor and psychiatrist, contended that ''our technology contributes to our ever-increasing fear of destruction and death.''[19] The significance of this, she argued, is that as people's physical ability to defend themselves against death gets smaller and smaller, their psychological defenses have to increase greatly to cope with the fear. ''Man cannot deny forever, nor can he pretend that he is safe.'' Naturally, this fear leads one to search for security, to be dependent, to find a provider, even if the provider is an aggressor.

Still, some Europeans protest the placement of U.S. missiles. As hostages might surrender their impulses to fight back in order to survive, Europe fears the United States as the threat to peace. As incredible as it seems, Europe often fancies that its strength lies in being weak—that parity with respect to nuclear weapons is dangerous. General Bernard Rogers, the former supreme NATO commander, reflected this attitude. Rogers said in 1986 that an annual 4 percent increase in Western budgets for tanks and other conventional equipment would enable the allies to "defend or contain" any Soviet threat. Faced with this NATO increase, he figured, the Kremlin would not attack.[20]

The Soviets have done their job well. The Europeans are forming identifications with the Soviets that are wholly unconscious on their part. The question that remains for U.S. policy makers is whether they will have the wisdom and courage to counter effectively the Soviet strategy.

Finlandization appears to be the immediate Soviet design for Western Europe. In the long run the Soviets would like to lead Europe to be more dependent on them, pointing to Finland as a kind of universal model of how capitalism and socialism can coexist peacefully.

Will the United States be able to utilize the psychological insights of the Stockholm Syndrome to counter the drift in Europe toward the Soviet Union?

The question of why the United States' European allies have moved away from their firm identification with the United States and her policies is a significant one.

Each honest politician and every U.S. citizen should be challenged when confronted by the list of examples showing Europe drifting toward an identification with the Soviet Union. They should be challenged to seek an explanation of why Europeans seem intent on creating a gulf between themselves and the United States at least as wide as the vast ocean that separates them geographically. They should be challenged to examine closely the relationship between Soviet intentions and strategy and the shift in European allegiance. They should be challenged when seeing an antiwar movement of some twenty million people who assist the Soviets in their aim to reduce Western European security to the point where it will appear that Europe has no alternative but to find security with Moscow. They should also be challenged by this alleged universal concern for humankind directed against "nuclear maniacs" and "ignorant men" like President Reagan and his advisers, while ignoring all evidence of Soviet expansionism.

Since the conclusion of World War II, the overriding U.S. policy in Europe has been to ensure the integrity and the liberty of European soil. The Soviet Union has always been, as it continues to be, in opposition to the implementation of that priority, with its own design for Europe waiting to the East.

The Soviet Union would like to control Western Europe as it does Eastern Europe.

> Arise, arise, great land
> For mortal strife arise.
> 'Gainst facist forces stand.
> 'Gainst the darkness we despise.
> Let noble anger seize you
> And surge up like a wave,
> The war you wage is holy
> All peoples shall it save.
>
> --Fighting Song of the Red Army

To the Soviets, their quest is like a holy war. Yet, even with the sure knowledge of Soviet desires, Europe courts the Soviet Union. She engages Moscow in parlay and trade. She seems to be confusing the Soviet Union with a partner, rather than perceiving it as an enemy.

Visits by Mikhail Gorbachev seem to underscore this confusion in Western Europe. During his visit to Great Britain, he received press coverage that might normally be reserved for royalty.

Margaret Thatcher, Britain's prime minister and a staunch anticommunist, emerged from her personal meeting with Gorbachev and announced to the waiting world that she would be able to work with him. "I like Mr. Gorbachev," she proclaimed. "We can do business together."[21]

Indeed.

In spite of her anticommunist sentiments, Mrs. Thatcher seems to have forgotten even the most recent of the many Soviet atrocities. She seems to have forgotten the downing of the civilian airliner, KAL flight number 007, by Soviet military aircraft. She seems to have forgotten the Soviet Union's cruel invasion of Czechoslovakia in 1968, crushing the Czechs' profound desire for freedom. Perhaps she has chosen, like so many of her colleagues, to concede Eastern Europe to Soviet domination. And what of the very recent falsehoods and deceptions that have come to light about the Soviet violations of the SALT II treaty and the dangerous coverup of the Chernobyl nuclear accident? Will she reassess her appraisal of the "man she can do business with" in light of these realities? Can one trust a matter as important as arms control negotiations with a nation that lies to its own people—and neighbors—about a hazardous nuclear accident ("What accident?").

I don't believe that Mrs. Thatcher's statement reflects any forgetfulness or lack of foresight on her part. I don't believe she has forgotten the reality of Soviet human rights abuses. Nor do I believe that she has forgotten the clear link between the Soviet Union and international terrorism.

I think that Mrs. Thatcher simply wanted to believe Mr. Gorbachev.

Many would suggest that Mrs. Thatcher's remark was a shrewd diplomatic maneuver. As a host to a visiting head of state, it was incumbent upon her to be graceful. Others would suggest that she was rising to the impressive public relations record of Gorbachev.

This public relations record includes the avowed intention to launch a year-long ban on nuclear testing, which was announced in Hiroshima on August 6, 1986, the forty-year anniversary of the U.S. bombing of that site. This public relations maneuver offends taste to the point of being grotesque. Less than a year later, Gorbachev promoted his proposal for the total abolition of nuclear weapons by taking out a full-page advertisement in the *New York Times*.[22]

Some might find solace in these explanations for Prime Minister Thatcher's statement. But they seem to fall short in trying to diminish the frightening incongruity of a leader of one of the world's great democracies, a woman we have been given to understand is the European leader closest to President Reagan, holding the torch of liberty in her one hand while in the other she holds out a welcome for the Soviet Union.

I stated that I believe that Mrs. Thatcher wanted to believe Gorbachev. Unconsciously, even she, a strong anticommunist, was moving in the direction of the Soviet Union. Chapter 7 examines the current Soviet leadership of Mikhail Gorbachev.

The strongest argument that this is so is that Mrs. Thatcher is not alone in her positive expression about the Soviet leadership. Her feelings and the cruel ignorance her sentiments suggest are epidemic all across Europe, from the radical Green party of West Germany to the established governments of all our NATO allies.

How can Europe be so effectively blindsided by the Soviets? How can Dorothy Solle, an influential activist in Germany's antimissile movement, declare that Europe must be free of atomic weapons "from Portugal to Poland," conveniently ignoring in her equation the Warsaw Pact countries with their Soviet missiles?[23] Or how can Petra Kelly, a leader of the Green party, suggest that "Europeans probably feel closer to the Soviet Union in a strange way because the Soviet Union lost twenty million people in the war. Young people of my generation are asking, 'Who dropped the bomb, really?' "[24]

It should be obvious that the Soviet arsenal amassed within seconds of Western Europe poses the greatest threat to Europe. It is the greatest of irrelevancies to point out "who was first" to drop the bomb, when those circumstances were so terribly different.

And what about Kinnock, leader of England's largest opposition party, who suggested during the 1984 Washington visit that "the possession of nuclear weapons does not add to our security, only to our vulnerability."[25] Who could explain such perverse logic?

Looking at Kinnock's remark, and those of other Labour party members, it is possible to see an example of the reversal of logic, which is one of the components of the Stockholm Syndrome.

He seems to suggest that a stronger defense, here in the form of nuclear arms, makes Europe more, rather than less, vulnerable to Soviet attack. This inversion of logic tends to cause an identification with the Soviets. Obviously, if a stronger defense cannot protect Europe, then Europe must turn to the Soviets, the real source of their vulnerability, to protect it. There are many other components of the Stockholm Syndrome, which I will delineate throughout this book.

All the statements previously listed reflect a reversal in logic. After all, each of these statements was made with apparent knowledge of Soviet military strength and firm resolve, clearly articulated as early as the 1960s by the "Missile Czar" under Krushchev, Leonid Brezhnev.

The party and the people will spare no effort to provide the glorious defenders . . . of our motherland with the most technically advanced weapons. We shall implement Lenin's appeals still more stubbornly and resolutely, be always on guard, guard the defense potential of our motherland like the apple of our eye, and multiply the strength of our glorious heroic Soviet armed forces.[26]

The armaments that Brezhnev talked of in the early 1960s, armaments that he stated would be to "defend the motherland," were then and have become even more powerful offensive weapons. These armaments created a strong hand for the Soviets. But an even stronger hand and a more powerful weapon is the psychological one that the existence of such armaments creates. The buildup of Soviet SS-20s is like a gun at the head of Europe. Yet like patients acting out a strange death wish, Europeans often refuse our weapons.

An arms buildup as the Soviets have engaged in for the past twenty years constantly heightens the atmosphere that can precipitate the effects of Stockholm Syndrome, for stress can lead to dependence and identification.

French psychologist Albert Memmi pointed out: "Ordinarily there are three or four elements that come together to establish an equation of dependence: the person who hopes to gain something from it, the object the person covets and the person who procures the object."[27] In my analysis I suggest that Europe's drift toward the Soviet Union reveals its own unconscious desire to covet security, freedom from stress, and survival at all costs.

Europe, feeling its growing vulnerability to the Soviet Union, unconsciously moves toward identification with the United States. Europe's feelings are as irrational and unconscious as those of hostage victims who not only identify with their captors but go so far as to perceive the police as their enemy. Listen again to the words of Petra Kelly: "Young people of my generation are asking, 'Who dropped the bomb, really?'" Isn't she suggesting that the United States threatens Europe more than, maybe even exclusively of, the Soviets?

Over the course of the past twenty years, U.S. policy makers have been increasingly at a loss to formulate an effective Soviet policy, because they have not taken into account the significance of the connection between Soviet strategy and the drift in European identification away from the United States. They have not grasped the causes of this phenomenon. They have not taken into account the applicability of the effects of the Stockholm Syndrome. To understand the behavior patterns of many hostages, like the ones in Washington who praised their Hanafi Muslim captors as "compassionate" after their thirty-six-hour spree of terror in the D.C. Capitol building, is to understand the psychological connection I speak of here.

By failing to understand this connection, our policy makers are moving the United States into increased isolation. This is exactly the position a Soviet strategist would want for the United States, isolated and alone in the fight against communism.

This growing isolation translates into a policy of concession. The United States is conceding Europe to Soviet influence. The signs are there to see. Kinnock's sentiments. Petra Kelly's words. Townsend's opinion. They hold the clue. They are strongly reminiscent of remarks made by the Beirut hostages who were exposing pro-Shiite sympathies in an attempt to identify best with their Arab captors. Such a tendency toward identification with a captor is a signal flag that the hostage is suffering from the effects of hostage syndrome.

Their words are reminiscent of Prime Minister Craxi's remarks immediately after the hijacking and murder aboard the *Achille Lauro* and again after U.S. military jets intercepted the Air Egypt plane attempting to carry the terrorists to safety. The underlying sentiment and the unconscious urges the words suggest remind us how the crew of the *Achille Lauro* hugged the Palestinian hijackers before they left the ship. And they also recall the crew aboard the hijacked flight from New York to Chicago who actually applauded the "decent conduct" of their Croatian captors after the ordeal had ended.[28]

Europe has, in very real psychological terms, become a hostage to the Soviet Union. Unconsciously, she is drifting away from an identification with the United States. Either represents significant strategic gains for the Soviets. They are happy to find a dependent for which to provide.

Until U.S. policy makers grasp the reality of this situation and appreciate its significance, they cannot formulate an effective policy to counter it and save Europe from its disastrous shift in identification. Until the United States counters the Soviet strategy and the European response, the United States' goal of effective and just world leadership will be significantly damaged.

*Captive Continent*

# 1

# *A Prelude*

I have stated that I believe that a clearly defined psychological dynamic is at work in the relationship between Europe and the Soviet Union. Now, the burden of establishing my case is before me. There are two parts to the argument. The first part seeks to show the rationale of imposing a psychology on nations. Doing this will require an examination of exactly what comprises the Stockholm Syndrome. Specific cases will be examined. The second task is to show that the Soviets have willfully gone about imposing this dynamic on the Europeans. This argument will be comprised of a survey of Soviet policy over the course of the past twenty years with attention being drawn to the connections between the Soviet policy and the psychological principle.

Despite amassing vast evidence to support a given interpretation of history, especially contemporary history, there is always a danger of interpreting events and moments of great complexity too simply. With this tendency to simplify comes the loss of the nuance and potential of events. We see this problem often in historical biographies that impose too tidy a perspective on an individual. Perhaps a childhood disappointment is noted and then given an exaggerated importance in order to prove the author's point. Or maybe it was a failed marriage. It doesn't matter; the point is that authors misuse subject's lives at times to prove their own points.

It is not the intention of this book to simplify the events of the past half century in Europe, or to simplify the relationship between East and West, or to simplify the personalities involved in the entire process. On the contrary, I believe that these events and people and this relationship are tremendously complex and subtle.

However, I do believe that the dynamic involved in these subtle and complex things is identifiable and straightforward.

As previously stated, my view requires that I present my argument along two parallel roads, bringing them together at the conclusion. One road is the European reaction to the Soviet Union. The other is the intention and strategy of the Soviets. The Soviet intention is world hegemony. Western Europe is a vital key to achieving that goal. If Europe is neutralized or identifies with the Soviets, the United States is isolated in the world community and is therefore limited in its ability to combat communist expansion. Europe has in the past, and probably would in the near future, counter a direct Soviet attack.

The Soviets were confronted with a dilemma: how to conquer Europe without violence, perhaps even with European support. The Soviets created a policy to accomplish their goal. The result has been to capture Europe more effectively than any Soviet tank rumbling through the streets of Paris ever could. The result has been to bring Europe to its knees in a clear captive–captor relationship with the Soviets. And the best part from the Soviet point of view is that for the most part the Europeans are reacting unconsciously and automatically. Just as students of the Stockholm Syndrome would expect.

I do not make this observation lightly. I recognize that the principles of psychology are more regularly applied to individuals. But my contention is, simply put, that the principles of psychology, carefully and systematically administered, can be generalized to apply to the group to encompass the nations of Western Europe.

This kind of thinking is legitimate, for we claim that some nations are greedy, others just. We sometimes impose the psychology of a nation on its leader and sometimes of the leader on the nation.

But more than a psychological diagnosis of an individual (or individual country), the hostage syndrome is a relationship. Therefore, we have the added advantage of being able to observe actions between the two parties instead of actions emanating from within just one.

Just as Patricia Hearst became Tania and held a gun as she participated in the Hibernia Bank robbery, so too has Europe begun its transformation from Western ally to hostage of the East.

# 2

# *The Stockholm Syndrome*

On Thursday, August 23, 1973, at approximately 10:15 in the morning, the usual calm of the Sveriges Kreditbank's routine in Stockholm, Sweden, was violently disrupted.[1] A slim, mustached man strolled into the bank and fired several rounds from a submachine gun into the ceiling of the bank. As the plaster and glass began to settle around the sixty or so occupants of the bank, the gunman called out in English, "The party has just begun."

The gunman proceeded to the tellers' cages. When he was confronted by a plainclothes policeman, he became frightened. He grabbed four hostages, Elizabeth Oldgren, age twenty-one, then an employee of fourteen months working as a cashier in foreign currency; Kristin Ehnmark, age twenty-three, then a bank stenographer in the loan department; Brigitta Laudblad, age thirty-one, an employee of the bank; and Sven Safstrom, age twenty-five, a new employee. He hustled all four into the bank vault.

There, for them, the party had indeed just begun. For the next 131 hours, nearly six days, these four were held hostage by a thirty-two-year-old thief, burglar, and prison escapee named Jan-Erik Olsson.

The bank vault itself was nothing more than an eleven-by-forty-seven-foot cell. One of Olsson's initial demands was the release from prison of his friend, Clark Oloffsson, age twenty-six. Once Oloffsson was released from the Norrkoping Penitentiary, he joined Olsson and the four hostages in the bank vault.

Beyond the initial and immediate trauma of the bank robbery attempt, which, by the way, was shared by everyone else who had been in the bank that morning when Olsson opened fire, the four hostages entered into a relatively long-term relationship with their captors.

It is the ramifications of this relationship that have the most bearing on the thesis of this book. For in those ramifications it is possible to recognize the tenor and tone of some of Europe's recent responses to Soviet aggression.

The most striking and ominous effect of this hostage–captor relationship is found in the hostages' feelings toward the police. Contrary to what might have been expected, it was discovered that the hostages, the victims of a terrible crime, feared the police more than they feared their captors. Let me emphasize this point. The hostages feared the legitimate authority—the authority that only hours before they had most likely respected and would have turned to—more than they feared the men holding the guns to their heads.[2]

As Kristin Ehnmark said in a telephone call to a television station when she urged the police to let the criminals go free, "The police are playing checkers with our lives." Even when Oloffsson himself put a call through to Prime Minister Olof Palme and threatened to kill Ehnmark in sixty seconds unless he was guaranteed safe conduct out of the country, she still perceived Palme as a greater threat to her survival than Oloffsson: "'The robbers are protecting us from the police,' she said. Even at the outset Oloffsson announced ironically, 'if anything happens to them, the police will be to blame.'"[3]

Unknown to the conversants Palme and Kristin, the police taped a forty-two-minute conversation between them. Here is a sample of their remarks:

*Kristin*:    I am scared that the police will attack and cause us to die.

*Prime minister*:    The police are there to protect you. They have not aggressively moved in.

*Kristin*:    Of course they can't attack; the robber's sitting in here and protecting us from the police.

Still later, Oloffsson spoke for the hostages' "interests":

The inspector gave a negative reply to a second request that had been made—permission for each hostage to receive a phone call from home. . . . So the girls have begun to feel that the police are looking to sacrifice them and are only looking for an excuse to justify the massacre later on. The girls believe that the police will make sure that it was we who started it and that the police simply defended themselves, so that afterwards they can regret that everyone was killed. The girls believe this because under no conditions can they get in touch with their relatives to tell them how the police are playing with their lives. We have it rather cozy here as long as the police leave us alone.

This message was scribbled on a blank bank form by the leader, Oloffsson, and left outside the door for the police to read. Strikingly, it entailed the idea that the police were the source of insecurity, uncertainty, frustration, and possible death. The hostages had begun to think like their captors.[4]

When the police finally flushed the hostages from the vault with tear gas, they shouted, "Hostages first. Hostages first." But for a long moment there was silence. The hostages were refusing rescue, despite the fact that only hours before they had ropes placed around their necks. These ropes, it was learned, were attached on one end to the safe deposit boxes in the vault and were to serve the purpose of strangulation or execution by hanging if the police persisted in the use of tear gas. The gas would render the hostages unconscious, causing their knees to buckle and their necks to snap. But this too was construed as a compassionate act in the eyes of the hostages: Oloffsson had an idea that fifteen minutes of tear gas caused permanent dementia, and he said he'd rather see his victims strangle than die that way.

Upon leaving the vault, Kristin shouted defiantly at the police, "No, Jan and Clark must go first—you'll gun them down if we do." Amazed, the police opened the outer door of the vault and made way for Oloffsson and Clark. After exiting, the group embraced one another like departing comrades, the women kissing their captors and Sven shaking hands with them.

Certainly survival, especially immediate survival, is a reasonable explanation for such behavior. Even some identification with the criminal is probably to be expected in such a situation. But what we see in this case, and others like it, is that identification with the captor continues for some variable period after the event.

In this case, for weeks after the robbery and kidnapping had ended, with all the hostages safely released and the robbers successfully captured, the hostages still could not puzzle out why they did not hate the robbers. In fact, Kristin Ehnmark, who suffered through the ordeal at least as much as the others, behaved most strangely after it was over. As she was being carried out of the vault on a stretcher, she smiled and called out to Oloffsson, "We'll see each other again." And while climbing into an ambulance Elizabeth expressed concern for the hostages. "I was thinking that whatever was being done for us should also be done for them," she said. Kristin's actions belied reports that she was the victim of a "temporary defense mechanism"; she subsequently broke off her engagement, which she had prior to the robbery, visited Oloffsson in jail, and eventually married him.

Her reaction, already one of stunning illogicality, was all the more illogical because, during the kidnapping, the police had used sensitive eavesdropping devices to monitor the activities inside the vault, and there was speculation that all the women had been raped. These reports were later denied. The traces of semen found on the carpet were, evidently, caused by one of the men's self-stimulation, as clarified in the later testimony.

Still, there were other strikes against the captors. Oloffsson, for his part, was unrepentant. He later told the police, "I was too soft; I should have shot one of the hostages." And when the drama had first begun, he strengthened his demand for a large ransom payment by choking one of the captives, whose fearful gasps were clearly audible over the phone. Despite these facts, Kristin and Elizabeth were compassionate when released. "Don't be too hard on them," they pleaded with police chief Gunnar Aastrom.

Because the entire drama had been covered live and extensively by the Swedish media, this form of hostage syndrome came to be known as the Stockholm Syndrome. Mindful of the hostages' compassionate reaction, one psychologist later referred to this happening as an instance of the "Poor Devil Phenomenon"; the victims had felt sorry for their captors.

A European daily composed the ironic headline, DARLING GANGSTER, and went on to describe the ordeal. The article commented on the decadent state of Swedish society in which captives showed great sympathy for men who made threats on their lives.[5] Moreover, the article focused on the captives' disrespect for law and order. One hostage was indignant about the newspapers' calling the incident a "drama" and their denunciation of the hostages as vicious criminals. The hostage in question chose to think of them as "polite, struggling human beings."

In comparing the information given from this incident to other hostages and of kidnap events, experts were able to draw some definite conclusions regarding the syndrome. First, the Stockholm Syndrome appears to be an automatic, unconscious emotional response on the part of the victim. Although not every prisoner succumbs to Stockholm Syndrome, it is an almost knee-jerk reaction to the initial trauma of becoming a victim. It is a reaction that calls the victim's entire reality framework into question.

Lennart Ljonggren, the physician in charge of the bank drama, commented that the hostages, on admission to the hospital, "remained in the first stages of reaction to catastrophe, characterized by overwhelming fright, fear of death, chaos and the elimination of all normal laws."[6] But oddly, even after this "first stage," the hostages could not change their appraisal of the captors. The syndrome has been observed to occur around the world; all kinds of persons are susceptible to it.

Before showing how the process has been at work in Europe, I will describe the process step-by-step to establish a firm understanding of how this relationship takes hold and develops.

First, the syndrome requires throughout the process an extremely high level of stress. Participants in a hostage drama are cast together in a life-threatening "extreme" environment where everyone involved must adapt in order to stay alive. The relationship that develops between the hostage and captor is a positive emotional bond born of the stress of the siege. It unites both hostage and hostage taker against all outsiders. It embodies the "us against them" world view. It is just one of many adaptive mechanisms to extremely dangerous situations.

A tremendous amount of research concerning the mechanics of this type of relationship has been done. This union, or identification, was observed in concentration camp inmates with their guards, kidnap victims, and political prisoners. Some long-term prisoners eventually adopted Nazi views on Aryan racial supremacy and the legitimacy of German expansionism. To date, there is no evidence to indicate how long the syndrome lasts. It seems to be an almost reflex reaction, like a knee responding to the tap of the doctor's rubber hammer. In different people, the level of response does vary. The bond between hostage and hostage taker is almost totally beyond the control of the victim.

In so many incidents the response seems automatic and human. The mechanism that sets off the hostage syndrome is typical for a survival situation. Many survival situations—whether they involve Korean or Vietnamese POWs, victims in concentration camps, hostages like the Americans in Iran, or persons skyjacked—produce feelings of belonging in the members of the group. This feeling is strengthened by a common danger that threatens the group: the out-group consisting of police and rescuers in general.

At first, the captive's adaptation is a defense against the demands of the harsh situation. But in time the submission comes willingly, the dependency is enjoyed, and the captor is revered as being both omnipotent and omnibenevolent. Prisoners not only respect the captors but at times will even imitate their behavior. I will consider more of these psychological elements in Chapter 3.

Perhaps no one is a more celebrated victim of hostage syndrome than Patricia Hearst. Her experience is a blueprint for all three stages of hostage syndrome: (1) sympathy for her captors; (2) fear of authorities; (3) recipient of her oppressor's love.

On a cool February evening in 1974, Patricia Hearst was kidnapped by a group of terrorists who called themselves the Symbionese Liberation Army (SLA). Her ordeal continued until February 1, 1979, when President Carter commuted her sentence with the pronouncement:

It is the consensus of all of those most familiar with this case that but for the extraordinary criminal and degrading experiences that the petitioner suffered as a victim of the SLA she would not have become a participant in the criminal acts for which she stands convicted and sentenced and would not have suffered the punishment and other consequences she has endured.[7]

Patricia Hearst was kidnapped by a woman, a black man, and a white man. She was bundled into the trunk of a car and taken to her first "prison." There she was shoved into a small closet and kept under guard, blindfolded, and gagged.

After studying her case and talking to Hearst for hours, Martin Orne, a psychiatrist and psychologist, told her that she had tremendous strength and resolve:

Miss Hearst, you really shouldn't feel embarrassed. Stronger men than you have cracked and cooperated with the enemy under less torturous conditions. The only thing surprising about all of this is that you are here with us today. You suffered severe sensory deprivation being tied up and blindfolded in that closet for so long. Other people subjected to such sensory deprivation would have given up the will to live. They just curl up and die, deprived of their senses for so long. You survived and that is remarkable in itself. You are a survivor.[8]

Short periods of sensory deprivation are mildly relaxing and pleasant; long periods are extremely harmful, however, producing time distortions, bizarre thoughts and images, and even hallucinations. Lacking sensory stimuli, the mind eventually turns inward, producing its own internal stimuli.

The experience of being kidnapped was a trauma that was powerful in making Patty vulnerable to her captors. Before she had realized that she was being put in a closet, she thought she would be buried alive. Consequently, she began to think of her captors as her saviors, because they "delivered" her from that death.

Patricia Hearst's statements were from the beginning supportive of the SLA. Her identification with them became stronger each day. She began to view the police and the FBI, even her family, as her real enemies.

Mom, Dad . . . Your silence definitely jeopardized my safety because it allows the FBI to attempt to find me, and Governor Reagan to make antagonistic remarks, with no response from you. I'm beginning to think that the FBI would rather that I get killed. It's the FBI, along with your indifference to the poor, and your failure to deal with the people and the SLA in a meaningful, fair way. I don't believe you are doing everything in your power, everything you can.[9]

She went on to say that she "no longer feared the SLA because they are not the ones who want me to die." After all, they were responsible for her deliverance from death!

Hearst was kidnapped by force, but her later identification with her brutal captors was voluntary. She identified with General Field Marshall Cinque and his pseudo-military troops. Her communiqués with the authorities revealed an empathy with the SLA and its causes, not to mention an appreciation of her own improvement through this ordeal.

The SLA, like other terrorists, denied freedom to their captive and transformed her into an object, in the name of freedom. Hearst perceived her captors as the "benevolent" ones, possessing the "sole truth" and the only "real" inspiration. In actuality, they denied their prisoner the freedom to decide what is good, useful, or important for her.

Hearst adopted her captor's vulgar vocabulary wholesale, proving her toughness with tough expressions. She concluded that bourgeois mentality is a "putrid disease," that all enemies, including her family, are "pigs and fascist insects," that bourgeois values, attitudes, and goals are "fucked up." Moreover she "belonged." She had a new name, new clothes, new friends, and a new vocation.[10]

The entire process of Patricia Hearst's captivity culminated in her "becoming" Tania and joining the SLA. She participated in a bank robbery, was convicted and sentenced to prison.

The most difficult question Patty Hearst had to answer during her trial was why, after she had been freed, did she still assist the Harrises in their escape from jail. She did this after all immediate threats to her life had been removed, after the stress of her captivity was over.

She could have replied that when an individual is under duress, so-called charismatic leaders, bosses, executives, companies, movements, ideologies, religion, even science (as Stanley Milgram's obedience experiments prove), and certainly dictators and kidnappers can become substitutes for individual conscience. The superego of the person thus internalizes the demands of outsiders.

To illustrate this tendency we can turn to countless hostage incidents in which, even weeks after the incident has ended, the hostages still feel sympathy for their captors, at the same time associating with them, on an emotional level, the blame and full responsibility for this horrible experience. A U.S. consul, after being held for ninety-five hours by Japanese terrorists, said, "I hope they might someday be people with whom I can sit down and have a cup of coffee while talking about politics."[11] Others speak of their captors with equal admiration. Such sentiments as, "They were dedicated men" and "Their sincerity should be respected" are frequent. Some even voice nostalgic fondness: "They were exceptionally polite, especially for terrorists."

After skyjackings, passengers and crews are often chock-full of blandishments. Two airline hostesses returned weapons to their skyjackers because they "felt sorry" for the poor devils who had been "so nice" and who, in their estimation, should be trusted and assisted. One U.S. airline hostess regularly visits "her" skyjacker in prison. She intends to wait out his term and marry him when he emerges from prison. As one of the hostages on a Dutch train taken by Moluccan terrorists said when he spoke to a psychologist after being released, "You have to fight feelings of compassion for them all the time."[12]

After two professional criminals held up a bank on a busy street in downtown Munich, they held seventeen hostages and insisted on a large ransom and safe passage from Germany. In an ensuing confrontation a hostage and criminal were killed entering the getaway car. The other prisoner was subdued before he could harm anyone else. The reaction? At the trial, an attractive young woman expressed pity for the defendant and claimed that she never felt threatened by him. She wished to help him any way she could. The judge reminded her of the criminal's violent record: He was a hardened criminal who had killed an innocent young girl and had threatened, intimidated, and terrorized decent citizens for many hours. She realized this but nevertheless insisted on staying in touch with the defendant and waiting for him to complete his jail sentence. Perhaps she would marry him, she said.

*Surviving the Long Night* is a book describing the hostage experience of Sir Geoffrey Jackson, British ambassador to Uruguay.[13] Jackson was kidnapped by the Tupamaros, and he was locked in the "People's Prison" for nine months in 1971. For the duration of the captivity he was pistol whipped and mistreated. But as time passed, he educated his captors, advising them about the distribution of food. He even redesigned the hoods they wore over their heads for disguises. In an all-too-common mood, he speculated about whether the brutality of his captors was created by their unfortunate environment in life or their defects in character.

The positive feeling toward his captors leads the hostage to perceive the police or his government in negative terms. When French archeologist Francoise Claustre was being held by Hissen Habre, a Moslem rebel, there was a breakdown in the negotiations for her release between the French government and Habre. When French television broadcasted an appeal by Claustre, who sobbed that the government was guilty of "inaction, cowardice and lies," she became an instant heroine in France. President Giscard d'Estaing agreed to pay the ransom.[14]

Twenty-seven-year-old Hartwig Faby, a hostage aboard a plane hijacked by South Moluccans, was forced to help dispose of the body of the murdered pilot of the plane. In spite of this experience, Faby, like many hijacking victims, began to identify with his captors during the long siege and to resent what he considered his government's heartlessness in letting the hostages suffer, rather than release other jailed terrorists as the hijackers demanded. "The 100 hours on the plane did create a sort of solidarity with the hijackers," he said. "We felt that we were all in the same boat, and that we had all been abandoned by the West German Government."[15]

Other incidents illustrate this ironic behavior even more forcibly. In 1977 eight Hanafi Muslims began a thirty-eight-hour spree of terror at the Islamic Center in Washington, D.C.[16] They took over several buildings; in the end one hostage was dead, four more were wounded by gunfire, and dozens were slashed by knives. This record, of course, doesn't even mention the psychological terror and humiliation the captives suffered. Altogether, 134 persons were threatened with decapitation. Yet in the second stage of this catastrophe the Hanafi leader Khaalis was freed, as promised by law enforcement authorities.

One woman from the besieged building recounted her paradoxical feelings. "I felt sorry for them [the captors]," she said. "They constantly had to take us to the bathroom. I don't think they meant to kill us.''[17] Another man held captive in the D.C. building described his captors with glowing warmth. Why? Because the Hanafis had shown consideration in letting him and other hostages use the bathroom.

Evidently, these feelings of compassion were contagious. Another testimony at the trial came from a B'nai B'rith secretary whom Khaalis allowed to answer his telephone, after first making sure she was not a Jew. She confessed to feeling a certain sympathy for her captor. ''He's very nice. He's basically a compassionate person.''[18] Others in the B'nai B'rith Building were subjected to violent anti-Semitic outbursts and brutal behavior. But this woman expressed gratitude and remarked how safe she had felt with the Hanafis during the siege. She felt no fear whatsoever, until she first saw the police. Her ''logic'' had told her that not only were the Hanafis compassionate, but that the police were stupid, irksome, even dangerous.

Eight of the Hanafis were jailed on multiple charges and held on $50,000 to $75,000 bail. But the three who took over the Islamic Center, where no one was injured and no shot was fired, were tried and freed under Washington's unusually liberal bail procedures. Because of the agreement with hostage negotiators, Khaalis was freed on his own recognizance after being charged with only a single count of kidnapping. Superior Court Judge Harold Greene thought that the deal was too lenient, but he acquiesced. A Democratic senator from Texas, Lloyd Bentsen, complained that ''Khaalis was at liberty even before his hostages were home.''[19] But a deal—even one with murderers—had to be honored.

A year earlier, a Serbo-Croatian ''nationalist'' group hijacked a jet full of passengers enroute from Chicago to New York. They took flight 355 on a global tour—to Canada, Newfoundland, Iceland, and finally Paris. At Ganeder, the terrorists released twenty-five hostages, a number of whom defended the character of their hijackers and their cause—Croatian independence from Yugoslavia. Some of them, apologetically, said they knew nothing of this cause before the hijacking. One passenger said: ''I wish them well. They had nothing against us but only wanted to get a story across.''[20] What's so terrible about being treated like a pawn? These sympathies are all the more incredible given the moral reality of the situation: The hostage isn't even a person to the criminal, but merely a means to his own ends.

Some of the hostages released at Ganeder admitted that they had come to respect the hijackers—among other reasons, because they had taken time during the flight to explain their motives. (This camaraderie reared its head in the D.C. incident as well: One captive spoke of the fellow feeling that existed between blacks and whites and Jewish and Christian prisoners held by the Hanafis at the B'nai B'rith offices.) At the end of the flight the captain came over the intercom and said with calm sincerity, "The experience is over for us, no one is hurt. But it is not over for the hijackers. For them the ordeal is just beginning. They have a cause. They are brave, committed people. Idealistic, dedicated people. Like the people who helped to shape our country. I think they deserve a hand." Incredibly, a round of applause followed, signaling the end of passenger enslavement—and perhaps cabin fever—aboard flight 355. As in the other adventures described, the threat to the hostages had already ended, and the passengers were still extolling the "good side" of the captors.

We should take a look at the rationale for not praising hostage takers.[21] To begin with, hostage takers display many of the characteristics of antisocial personality. This means that they often possess inadequate conscience development—they simply have not internalized ethical values to the point where those values act as guides to their behavior. As a result, these captors are often lacking in a sense of responsibility, and so they view hostages as mere pawns. Moreover, typical hostage takers believe that the penalties for crime don't apply to them. But the defining characteristic of this personality—and the biggest problem of all for hostages and negotiators—is a lack of feeling in interpersonal relationships. In short, captors view hostages as instruments, objects or means to their own political or financial ends. These considerations make it all the more amazing that hostages are ever sympathetic to their captors. One hijack victim aboard the TWA 847, Peter Hill, was asked to recall the character of his captors. "They're animals, absolute animals. . . . The only thing they understand is strength."[22] Perceptions of hostage takers range over a very wide spectrum.

Other incidents exhibit hostage syndrome in less dramatic fashion. For almost a week, 149 passengers were prisoners of the Popular Front for the Liberation of Palestine, aboard a U.S. plane that was hijacked to the Desert of Jordan. Interestingly, passengers aboard this plane curtailed the development of hostage syndrome among some of their fellow hostages. While some passengers were passing time by talking in a "friendly fashion" with the Palestinian physicians and female guards, others grew angry and reprimanded them for "fraternizing with the enemy." Aboard this truly bizarre flight—during which one little girl's birthday was celebrated and others jumped rope to pass the time—other splits developed. Some passengers joined the

Palestinians in expressing both anti-U.S. and anti-Jewish feelings. But as we will see, Stockholm Syndrome requires a deeper identification between captor and captive. While there was a modicum of playful humanity on board, a relationship based on sympathy and understanding never achieved a foothold.[23]

A similar situation existed aboard the TWA 847 hijacking of June 1985. One of the captors asked the stewardess, Uli, to sing to him. She obliged with soft, German versions of "Patty Cake, Patty Cake" and Brahm's "Lullaby." Kurt Carlson recalled that she sounded like a mother singing to a family. Another captor stopped beating Carlson, put his arm around him, and said, "I love you. I meant not to kill you." Their relationship was more human from that point on. But not all the conditions necessary for Stockholm Syndrome occurred, and Carlson's animosity did not wane.[24]

On September 5, 1986, four men dressed as security guards boarded Pan Am flight 073 in Karachi. A familiar scenario began to unfold. The machine-gun-wielding men subdued members of the flight crew and initiated a torturous sixteen-hour episode of terror, and finally mass murder, by announcing, "Ladies and gentlemen, please lean forward in your seats with hands on head or you will be shot."[25]

This has become standard operating procedure for terrorists seizing aircraft. And the range of psychological responses among the victims are also commonplace. Some passengers are incredulous, some defiant, some tearful, some compliant. The sympathy that victims feel for their captors often doesn't flourish to the point where Stockholm Syndrome takes root.

Stockholm Syndrome really didn't occur aboard flight 073. The cards were stacked against such an occurrence. For hostage syndrome to occur, there must be ample time and even a bit of amiability between conqueror and conquered. Without these two ingredients the victim cannot identify with or put himself in the place of the aggressor. In the cabin of the Pan Am jet the mood alternated between relaxation, boredom, anxiety, and ultimately, horror. Limited time—and hostility—precluded the development of a bond between the gunmen and passengers.

On closer inspection, however, the seeds of sympathy had begun to take root. For one, some of the passengers perceived the hijackers as "low-key" people during much of the episode and even noted how they "bantered" with their victims. One Ulrich Sorenson, a Danish development official, recalled how "polite" the hijackers were. Another woman, referring to how the attackers had allowed sandwiches and soft drinks to be distributed, concluded, "We were treated very well."[26]

These responses ought to strike disinterested observers as incredible. Consider that the hijackers allowed passengers to go to the bathroom only on the condition that they crawl on all fours. Consider also that they collected passports for the sole purpose of finding a U.S. citizen to execute! These details suggest viciousness and depravity—anything but "polite" treatment. After one of the captors assured the passengers, "We have nothing against you people"—but only wanted to be flown to Cyprus to obtain the freedom of three Palestinian hijackers who were sentenced to life imprisonment—they killed Rajesh Kumar, a Californian who had only recently become a U.S. citizen. One of the men stripped off his shirt to reveal his chest and grenade-bedecked his waist à la Rambo. Despite the showy brutality of these men, there is a perverse logic that makes captives identify with them.

Captors often spend time endearing themselves to their "congregation." This happened in Karachi. A Pan Am passenger recalled how the "tall and handsome" leader sat down to apologize for his behavior. "I really prefer to drink, meet girls, dance and enjoy life," the leader said. "I'm sorry, I don't like to do this, but I have no country."[27] Personal confessions like these tend to put a human face on an otherwise ugly situation and facilitate transformation. This is also true of press conferences that allow hostage takers to air their views. Hostages, and the general public, might be led to see these aggressors as nice men or sincere people. Instead of being seen as brutal gunmen who terrorize people, they are seen as victims who are without choice in accepting this violent manner of furthering their cause. Forgotten in these humanizing exchanges is the constant humiliation of being held prisoner, the terror of a gun held to the temple, and the blood that eventually flows.

The public analogue of Stockholm Syndrome can befall the viewer who listens to terrorist press conferences. Said William Henry of *Time Magazine*, "If you do a press conference with hostage-takers you allow them to humanize their image. Even if they're making outrageous demands, they have the opportunity to present themselves as victims."[28] Here captors show their "humanity" not just to the hostages but to the world.

It is simply false to argue, as some have, that hostages are not swayed by the personality of their captors. Stockholm Syndrome is more likely to occur if the perpetrator is handsome, has a cavalier personality, and is well-spoken.

After the release of the TWA 847 hostages, Don Kladstrup of ABC News in Paris remarked, "17 days is not enough to have developed Stockholm Syndrome."[29] This statement flies in the face of many hostage incidents, like the Stockholm bank event itself, which lasted only six days. The length of time required does vary. But it can certainly occur in seventeen days. In the same vein, the remarks of Father Thomas Dempsey, a hostage aboard the TWA flight, should be viewed with skepticism. Dempsey felt that "the whole Stockholm Syndrome is ludicrous. . . . It seems to me to be a fabrication of writers' minds, rather than reality."[30] But fabrication it surely is not. The evidence is empirical: frequent hostage episodes and similar behavior patterns that occur again and again. Perhaps Father Dempsey and Kladstrup were confusing Stockholm Syndrome with brainwashing.

The hostage syndrome is not the result of brainwashing. Although in many kidnappings, and most especially in politically motivated kidnappings, there is some attempt to reeducate, success or failure has little to do with the effects of the hostage syndrome. In his *Thought Reform and the Psychology of Totalism*, Robert Lifton stresssed the totality of brainwashing, the attempt to completely change the captive through reeducation.[31] Most hostage situations do not aim at this kind of 360-degree change, nor does the occurrence of the Stockholm Syndrome need the emotional, intellectual, and physical pressures found in brainwashing procedures.

The victim identifies with the hostage taker. Identification makes its first appearance as a mechanism of defense: That is, it is a means by which the self adapts to the demands of a dangerous situation. This adaptation obviously promotes the self's safety and chances of survival. But this occurs with or without the hostage taker's specific attempts to bring it about. Because of this identification, the victim's attitudes and actions become congruent with the hostage taker's. As we'll see, the identification is the key to the hostage syndrome, not any attempt at reeducation.

The hostage syndrome is an automatic response, primarily to the stress of the situation. Freud said, "A traumatic situation is an automatic determinant of anxiety: the essence of this experience of helplessness on the ego's part in the face of excitations that cannot be dealt with."[32] The organism defends against the trauma of being a victim. But what specifically happens to a person confronted with the stress of an extreme situation?

One study shows that sudden stimuli—like the shooting of a gun nearby or the clicking of a rifle bolt heard while blindfolded—cause a "startle response."[33] This response is innate, and it seems to precede the emotions of fear and anxiety. The intensity of anxiety is variable and depends on differences in the perceivers themselves. Research reveals, however, that when any organism is thrown into a catastrophic situation—a situation in which it cannot cope with the demands of its environment—it will feel a threat to its existence or essential values. The catastrophic condition described here is similar to the condition in which hostages and prisoners find themselves in the initial stages of their captivity. Every individual has a threshold beyond which additional stress makes the situation catastrophic.

Studies of soldiers who have broken down in battle substantiate this last point. And the function of various defenses of the soldiers against stress—defenses like self-reliance to the point of believing themselves invincible, compulsive activities, faith in the strength of God or their leader—is to protect the individual from extreme conditions. These facts about stress and its effects show how a person may very well respond to extremity by identifying with a captor or leader.

According to some observers, the trauma of a hostage situation forces hostages into a regression of sorts, pushing them back into a more primitive emotional state, one that is more in line with their immediate vulnerability and dependency. These observers suggest that victims are forced into an emotional state like that of a young child, a child whose entire world view is controlled by the closest authority figure, usually a parent.

The initial trauma of the situation so confuses the ego's normal notion of a reality framework that it adapts by seeking a reality framework more in line with the external reality. It is this adaptation that leaves the victim in a childlike emotional state.

A study of the men involved in the *Pueblo*—the U.S. gunboat crew that was captured by the North Koreans and incarcerated—shows that men who maintained a faith in their commanding officer, their religion, or their country coped much more successfully with the anxieties of their incarceration. More than half the captives in that situation reported significant anxiety due to the unpredictability of their treatment. Nonetheless, various strategies of coping prove to be effective in combating the anxiety. One person in the group even reported that his faith in his captain was like his faith in God.

Other captives have defended against stress by believing in a powerful, loving deity. Sven, a captive in the Stockholm bank vault, not only concluded that Oloffsson was a "very nice man," but added that "each show of friendliness on his part reinforced his leadership," and "when he treated us well, we could think of him as an emergency God."[34] Kurt Carlson, an army reserve officer aboard the hijacked TWA 847, recalled repeating the words of the twenty-third Psalm while he was being beaten within a inch of his death:

I felt the heels of the hijacker's leather shoes grinding into the muscles of my back and shoulders, and I gave them more noise, although I could have taken it without a sound. I was praying that I'd feel no more pain; I have always been afraid of pain. I began repeating over and over the line of the twenty-third Psalm: "Yea though I walk through the valley of the shadow of death, I will fear no evil, for Thou art with me, Thy rod and Thy staff, they comfort me." My body felt numb.[35]

Many hostages were able to cope with extremity through faith, while for others faith provided no defense against pain. The remark of Moorhead Kennedy, a hostage held in Iran for 444 days—"There are not many atheists among hostages"—is therefore without force for persons of agnostic temperament.[36]

Coping by faith is but one of many defenses that have aided persons in extreme situations. These defenses, of course, are necessary to mitigate overwhelming stress. Said eighteenth-century German philosopher Spinoza, "Each thing in itself desires to preserve its being."[37] But to "preserve one's being" in extremity requires not only a certain kind of activity but a radical shift in one's sense of self.

Certainly, the initial trauma of becoming a victim causes unbearable stress. Reports in concentration camps show that the first stage of captivity, the first encounter with horror, immersed prisoners in a world of pure terror. This encounter would disintegrate—literally "pull apart"—one's person. When writers like Terrence Des Pres and Bruno Bettelheim described the camp experience, they mentioned that the vast majority of inmates die soon.[38] And Viktor Frankl, in his book *Man's Search for Meaning*, mentioned that a dulling of the emotions is necessary in order to snap back from initial trauma.[39] "The new prisoner undergoes a kind of emotional death," said Frankl, "and this is a necessary mechanism of self-defense." One might react to this by saying that most hostage experiences are not really as severe as the concentration camp or POW experiences endured by many people. This is a good objection.

In terms of duration, frequency of physical harm, death, and malnutrition, hostages on a ship or plane do not undergo the same trials as survivors in the death camps, the Gulag, or even POWs in such places as Japan, Vietnam, and Korea. In fact, the discrepancy between the experiences was the subject of some gallows humor. One survivor of Buchenwald was a passenger aboard the plane skyjacked to the Desert of Jordan. Fellow passengers were complaining of their maltreatment at the hands of the Palestinians when she screamed, "Compared with what I lived through this is a Hilton Hotel."[40] Not many replied.

But with respect to stress, these situations are more similar than we would expect. The stress and the feelings of uncertainty due to what Frankl called "a provisional existence"—an existence of unknown limit—are remarkably similar. Moreover, since stress is largely a subjective phenomenon, in that its intensity is dependent on the person, there is no reason to claim that the quality of captivity in a concentration camp is different in kind than captivity for a week, a month, or a year (as in Iran). As we will see, there are stages of hostage syndrome that are similar to the kinds of stages that apply to life in a concentration camp.

In understanding the process of coping in a hostage situation, it is useful to review part of Sigmund Freud's structural theory of the personality. According to the Freudian theory, the ego, governed by the reality principle, assumes a controlling function over the id and the superego. In effect, what is occurring is a constant mediation among the demands of reality, the instinctual demands of the id, and the moralistic demands of the superego.

The ego in a healthy personality is dynamic and resourceful; it brings into play a whole range of psychological defense mechanisms that are described in Anna Freud's *The Ego and the Mechanisms of Defense*.[41] These defenses apply to all sorts of scenarios in which they are needed. The purpose of the defense mechanism is basic and agreed upon by the entire spectrum of experts—to protect the self from hurt and disorientation.

When the self is threatened—as it is to some degree in almost any stress situation—the ego must adapt. It is the ego that enables the personality to function even during the most painful experiences, like the death of a loved one or being taken hostage by an armed, anxious stranger. The hostage wants to survive. The healthy ego seeks a means to achieve the goal of survival. The impressive variety of ways in which the ego copes shows a lot about the stress of extreme situations and what they can do to the self.[42] In addition, these coping strategies show us what human beings can do to alter their reality. Coping behavior seems to confirm Dostoyevsky's definition of the human as "a being who can get used to anything."[43]

There are two widely held attitudes about coping behavior: (1) Individuals in extreme situations are completely powerless to influence their fate; (2) Only barbaric persons, especially inmates in concentration camps, can survive extreme situations. Both of these beliefs fly in the face of the evidence about defense mechanisms and Stockholm Syndrome. The beliefs are simply not based on a careful study of survivors of catastrophic situations.

A survey of coping behaviors used in concentration camps reveals a great deal about inmate behavior that can profitably apply to the behavior of all hostages. The method behind the survey was to locate concentration camp survivors, all nineteen of whom were healthy—able to function in work or family situations—and willing to talk. The discoveries made are similar to those made in Tim Wells's book about the U.S. hostages in Iran, *444 Days*.[44] Both studies report the day-to-day survival activities of prisoners.

One frequent coping strategy might be called the mobilization of hope, believing that ultimately the outcome will be tolerable and suffering will end. As we have seen, this strategy is effective for some captives in defending against the pain of captivity. But for others, like Douglas Valentine, an American in a Japanese POW camp in World War II, religious belief provided no protection. What especially pained Valentine was the death of his friend Bobby: "I stopped believing in God when Bobby died. Corny as it may sound, I just couldn't understand why God would take a truly decent person [shot in battle] while allowing evil men to go on living. . . . God doesn't decide who'll live and who'll die."[45] Two interesting elements of Valentine's beliefs tell us why he couldn't believe and couldn't therefore mitigate the pain of his own captivity. The first element is "God doesn't decide"; all evidence suggested to him that God doesn't intervene in human affairs. The second element concerns the old philosophical problem of evil. The problem is, if God is an all-powerful and loving being, why would he allow evil to occur, in this instance the suffering of an innocent human being?[46]

Another notable defense against terror is coping by defying and actively resisting danger. Defiance was practiced by Jacob, a concentration camp survivor, who adopted the attitude that he would be killed by the SS anyway, and so he might as well die with dignity. He was active in the camp underground, and he paid no attention to danger while he worked to save other inmates and watch over "new transports" into the camp. A psychologist later told him that he underestimated powerful men and that he could cause harm to himself by failing to perceive danger. He coped through defiance and survived the camp.[47]

An army attaché and hostage in Iran, Colonel Leland Holland, put the same strategy to work. During an intense interrogation period by the Iranian guards, Holland recalled:

There were a couple of times they came in with guns and put them to my head. After a while I was numb. I was beat. I was tired. I was exhausted [the interrogation lasted thirty-six hours]. I said, "Bullshit, pull the fuckin' trigger." I was almost at the point of wishing they would. . . . I'd seen Mashala (a Mujihanin guerilla) pull a few tricks when he was bringing people in. He'd have a guy sitting there blindfolded, put the gun up to his head, point it toward the sky, and pull the trigger. Well, they hadn't gotten what they wanted out of me, and I thought that that was what they were going to do. I thought, "they're not going to kill me. They're going to bust my eardrums." And I said, "pull the fuckin' trigger."

But they didn't do anything. When they didn't, I thought, "Aha! There's something going on here." It was like catching a second wind. I had challenged them on it and they didn't follow through. My battery was charged up again. I felt renewed.[48]

Strong defiance cannot work for all persons. A defense mechanism will only effectively mediate between a person and his hostile environment if the person can bear stress. Some persons in Iran and other extreme situations have had so little experience with violence that even being handcuffed breaks them down. Solzhenitsyn observed that some of the prisoners in the Soviet camps were so genteel, and their standards of behavior so high, that all the Soviet police had to do was curse them and they'd be upset.

Another frequent coping strategy in extremity is what some might call focusing on the good. This strategy is based on the idea that a person always has a choice of what to focus on—good or bad, ugly or beautiful, half full or half empty. Inmates at Dachau were known to focus on minor gratifications—like getting through the food line without receiving a beating; this mental act of focusing allowed them mentally to bury the deeper tragedies of camp life.

Consular Officer Richard Queen, a captive in Iran who was dismissed in July 1979 because of his worsening multiple sclerosis, discovered a surprising source of inspiration in his early days of captivity. Among other things, he would joke with the Iranian militants in an attempt to humanize his own environment. He recalled his first location in captivity: "I was in one of the upstairs bedrooms. I remember we faced the mountains in the distance. The first snows had come on those mountains, and it was a very beautiful sight. . . . Then, as evening rolled around, I remember watching the sunset. With the mountains it was nice, real beautiful."[49]

Another adaptation to the brutality of imprisonment is psychological removal. This involves developing ways of not feeling, insulating oneself from outside stress so that "I'm not here." We have already noted how Kurt Carlson attempted to remove himself from his brutal beating by taking refuge in the twenty-third Psalm.

Bruno Bettelheim coped with his life in a concentration camp by gathering data about the behavior of his fellow prisoners in extreme situations. He wrote:

> The study of these behaviors was a mechanism developed by him [Bettelheim] ad hoc in order that he might have at least some intellectual interests and in this way be better equipped to endure life in the camp. His observing and collecting of data should be considered as a particular type of defense developed in an extreme situation. . . . It was developed to protect himself against a disintegration of his personality. It is, therefore, a characteristic example of a private behavior.[50]

Bettelheim was hampered by having no paper or writing instruments and so relied on memory. However, "as time went on, the enhancement of my self-respect due to my ability to continue to do meaningful work despite the contrary efforts of the Gestapo became even more important than the pasttime."[51] He was slowed by malnutrition, which he feared would keep him from remembering his data. But he did remember. And even if he hadn't, the intellectual exercise would still have served as a means to the end of intellectual removal.

Denial strategy works wonders in shielding inmates from the total shock of their imprisonment.

As a POW in Hanoi from 1967 to 1973, Admiral William Lawrence survived with the help of this strategy. Lawrence, like Bettelheim, was able to achieve a subject–object split. Miraculously, he didn't let the enslavement of his bodily self affect the rigor of his mental discipline. Said Lawrence:

> One time they put me in an isolation cell we called Calcutta, after the Black Hole of Calcutta. They caught me communicating [with fellow prisoners] and they were determined to break my spirit. They didn't put many P.O.W.s in Calcutta—in fact, I know of only one other guy who was there. It was a dark cell, probably about six feet square. It had a tin roof and during the day the sun would beat down on that. I figure the temperature went up to 120 degrees in the daytime. And the problem that I had was a very bad heat rash. My body was completely covered with heat sores—they advanced from a rash to big sores. I was completely immobile because it was so painful. I said, "I've got to get some mental activity going here."
>
> That's when I started writing poetry. I could actually see the lines of poems in my head. Here I was, totally immobile, just lying completely flat and I don't know how

many days it took me—probably two weeks of fifteen or sixteen hours a day of total concentration—and at the end of that time I completed this perfect Iambic pentameter poem. It was a dark room and I could see those lines. The experience really gave me an appreciation of the mental capacity that you have that very very few people ever utilize.[52]

Lawrence achieved a separation from his world, a perfect separation of his physical from his mental self. It was as if he had said, What they're doing to me is happening to my objective self, me as "object" and body—but not to my subjective self, my "person."

Patty Hearst, realizing that she was being branded a common criminal after the Hibernia Bank robbery, said that she preferred to be "numb" and carry out SLA activities by "rote." Otherwise, she couldn't cope with the constant stress of imminent death due to a siege by the FBI. One inmate at Dachau remarked: "When I think of all the feelings we block; if you felt too much, you felt bad. To feel was to feel unpleasant, better not to feel at all."[53]

Strategies of removal include several subcategories. Intellectualization is a very good way of withdrawing from the impact of reality. In extremity persons sometimes attempt to decrease the threat of death by withdrawing into considerations of immortality. In Tolstoy's *The Death of Ivan Illych*, Ivan lies on his deathbed, recollecting the episodes of what he fears is a wasted, meaningless life. Suddenly, as if being thrown a life preserver, he awakens to "the light," to the possibility that death may not be final, that his spirit may not die.[54]

The various strategies of psychological removal have in common lifting oneself from the world of the senses, somehow transcending the threatening physical world, and escaping to another realm where physical realities, like pain and death, do not apply.

Perhaps the most basic coping strategy of all is the will to survive. Although this may seem trivially true, it turns out to be the most important aspect of coping. Those who don't last through captivity often fail to last because they simply lose the will to live.[55] After being raped by Cinque, the "Grand Marshall of the SLA," Patty Hearst realized her single-minded goal:

If I somehow survived, perhaps those rapes would have saved my life. My thoughts at this time were focused on the single issue of survival. Concerns over love and marriage, family life, human relationships, my whole previous life, had become, in SLA terms, bourgeois luxuries. No matter how hard I turned it over in my mind, I came to the bleak conclusion that there was no one out there who could help me; I was on my own.[56]

The coping behaviors we have examined so far are undertaken and of necessity are conscious and strategic. But other adaptations to extremity are unconscious. Hostage syndrome is one such adaptation, and to this phenomenon we now turn.

According to William Sargent, a psychologist who examined many of the hostages in Iran, the first phase of hostage captivity might be called the hysteroid phase, a phase affecting not only captives but their captors as well. In this state the brain—a mechanical computer obeying precise laws—is under great stress and begins to show extreme excitement. But this is generally followed by a progressive inhibition of the brain activity. The net result of this phase? The individual's "computer" becomes so scrambled that he starts to believe statements whether true or not. Statements he would normally question he now believes. His critical faculties are now on hold; even the greatest absurdities can become firmly held viewpoints. Fear has a great deal to do with this condition.

"Fear arises from a weakness of mind and therefore does not appertain to the use of reason," Spinoza once said.[57] But we can ask of Spinoza—and of others who recommend that we deliver ourselves from the bonds of fear to the freedom of reason—how should one act in a catastrophic situation? How can one ignore the three *d*'s—debility, dread, and dependency—that extremity causes? Can the initial shock of captivity be overcome by dedication to reason? The evidence bearing on the behavior of people in extremity suggests that the experience is too overwhelming.

In the face of danger, dreaded feelings of helplessness and absurdity are bound to arise. The nature of this anxiety—which hostages know well—is best understood if we ask, Exactly what is threatened in the experience that produces this anxiety? The threat goes to the core of the persons threatened. Threatened are their self-esteem, their experience of themselves as persons, their own feelings of having worth. In a word, their entire selves—including life itself—are at stake.

The positive statements of victims of hostage syndrome mask a tremendous inner turmoil. It is understandable that their perceptions be turned "upside down." After all, the deep-seated fear of death is constantly present in most hostages.

Just how deeply the fear of death tears into a captive can be measured by the defenses against death that they adopt. Persons feeling great anxiety about death manage to lie to themselves about it. Thoughts about death are pushed into the background of our minds and covered over. This process Sigmund Freud called the "Splitting of the Ego in Self-defense.''[58] In this process the ego represses the unpleasant thoughts arising from the external or internal world. The only way to achieve this denial is by effecting a "psychic split."

One manner of eliminating or at least mitigating death anxiety is by identifying with the agent of death, for instance a hostage-taker. In this respect identification has more than a little in common with denial and self-deception.

The diary of Anne Frank reveals how the Frank family denied death to the extent of not believing in the possibility of their own death, not believing in Auschwitz and the gas chambers. The family wanted their life to go on as it had, without having to separate and go into hiding. In effect they were saying, What is happening around us cannot happen to us. The fear of death seems to carry denial with it, not to mention extreme terror.

During the worst prison riot in U.S. history, in February 1980, more than seventeen correctional officers were taken hostage at the penitentiary of New Mexico near Santa Fe.[59] The environment for the hostages was described as "chaotic beyond belief." Much of the prison was in darkness due to a failure of electrical power during the riot. Dense smoke filled the corridors, and only silhouettes could be seen. Six inches of water were on the floor due to broken pipes. Bodies of inmates who were either beaten, killed, or who had taken drug overdoses were scattered throughout the institution. How were the hostages? Their state was later described as combining feelings of helplessness, existential fear, and sensory overload.

Correctional officers described their experiences as absolutely different from any ordinary experience. For one, all the captives experienced a feeling of total helplessness.

The officers' experience of existential fear was also profoundly different from anything they had previously felt. They were certain they would be killed by one of the roving execution squads carrying glass, sticks, pipes, and knives.

High sensory input or sensory overload also seemed to characterize their ordeal. They could hear the screams of inmates being tortured and murdered. Aside from the smoke and water, the winter chill came in through shattered windows. The death squads traveling in packs issued threats of violence and death. Each new scream produced a new startle reaction, as did noise of something being destroyed.

The experiences of the New Mexico hostages confirmed a point about the experiences of prisoners of war: No amount of preparation can make one ready for a frightening hostage situation. Persons held hostage under such conditions for as little as four to eight hours can later exhibit signs of a lasting neurosis.

The helplessness that the New Mexico captives experienced was similar to feelings of concentration camp prisoners. In both cases the behavior of the inmates was characterized by regression to childlike or infantile levels of behavior. For one, men and women in camps were abnormally preoccupied with food and excretory functions. Infants, of course, have similar preoccupations, so the comparison suggests that men and women respond to extremity by "regression to, and fixation on, pre-Oedipal stages." Bruno Bettelheim argued that since inmates were "forced to wet or soil themselves"—as infants do—it was impossible "to see themselves as fully adult persons anymore."[60] Indeed, one of the favorite pastimes of the *Kapo* (a person originally a prisoner but made into a guard) was to stop prisoners from using the latrine.

It has been convincingly argued that as a result of this kind of treatment, many survivors suffered a disintegration of self and were reduced to infantilism, a condition of complete and childish dependency on their master. Bruno Bettelheim showed how terror can force men and women to "live like children, only in the immediate present" and even to adapt to some of the values of their oppressors. Again, the tendency is to assume that the camps were dramatically different from hostage situations. But many hostage incidents, like the New Mexico prison riot, reflect the same inmate helplessness and dependency of the infantile state.

Concentration camp prisoners were ready to obey Gestapo authority; they firmly believed that the rules set down by the Gestapo were desirable standards of behavior, at least in the camp situation. Prisoners even rationalized their own brutality against other prisoners and the brutality of the Gestapo as well. They attributed benevolent motives to the Gestapo, even when their behavior was vicious. Like many hostages, they came to "understand" their captors. They felt they were following their own life goals and values, whereas they really were accepting Nazi values as their own.

On board the TWA 847 passengers were dominated as if they were children. The guard that Kurt Carlson called "Hitler" ordered that no one talk and told everyone to put their heads down in their laps and clasp their hands over their heads. Carlson called this the "847 position," which the hostages would remain in for six hours, like school children having to lay their heads on their desks. This was especially torturous, since the position essentially is like wearing a blindfold; with their heads down, no one knew what would happen next.

Aside from the screams of a guard yelling, "One American must die, one American must die," passengers could hear the cries of Robert Stethem, the navy diver who would eventually be murdered, being kicked and stomped. And the air inside the plane had become hot and stale. It also smelled, since "not everyone had been able to stifle nature's call."[61]

Bettelheim stressed that the infantile behavior in the camps was not peculiar to a few individuals but was a mass phenomenon. Many captives developed characteristics typical of infancy or early youth. The captives were tortured "in a way a cruel and domineering father might torture a helpless child."[62] Moreover, the prisoners were forced to address each other as "thou," which in Germany is practiced only among very young children. They were not permitted to address one another with the many titles to which middle- and upper-class Germans are accustomed. On the other hand, they had to address the guards in the most obsequious manner. This controlled depersonalization goes a long way toward eliminating persons' self-respect and forcing them back to a time when they hadn't yet attained individuality; back to infancy.

Captives, once depersonalized and robbed of all humanity, become things; so the logic of such treatment is crystal clear: You degrade captives so it is then easier to mistreat and possibly kill them. Once you see your opponent as human, it is harder to kill them. As Hannah Arendt said, "it is the glance in the eyes" that makes killing difficult.[63]

The depersonalization of a hostage incident occurs almost immediately. Once a trauma or event that initiates the Stockholm Syndrome occurs, there appear to be three distinct phases in the syndrome.

In the first phase, there are positive feelings on the part of the hostages toward their captors. These feelings mirror the feelings of a child in a parent–child relationship.

Second, when identification is set, the hostage begins to have distinct negative feelings toward the police or other government authorities. The hostages are highly inclined to understand, cooperate, and even love their momentary dictators to defend against the thought of their own destruction. Thus, we find many hostages attempting to negotiate with their enforcement officials, like those in the Stockholm case. Instances are frequent in which the hostages have shielded the captors from fire, have warned the captors of potential danger, or have even refused to exit buildings after captors have released them.

Finally, in the third phase there is a reciprocity on the part of the captor toward the hostage. A relationship develops. It is this third phase that lends the most hope for the successful resolution of a hostage crisis. If the positive feelings of the captor toward the hostage can be induced by the hostage's behavior or the intervention of a negotiator, then there is a strong possibility that seeing his victim as a full human being, he will be unable to truly hurt him.

To counteract this feeling, captors often force their prisoners to lie face down on the floor or to stand spread-eagle, face against the wall. Talk has developed about terrorists' plans to put hoods over the heads of their captives to keep them totally isolated, so the transference process will not interfere with their mission.[64] Hostage negotiators try to counter these dehumanizing tactics with their own stock of "humanizing" approaches to negotiation. For example, negotiators use hostages' names while speaking to the captors: "How is Sherry?" or "Is Bill hungry?" Besides this kind of humanizing, the negotiators endeavor to get the prisoners and captors involved in some sort of communal activity. Instead of sending in ready-made sandwiches, negotiators might send the ingredients, like bread, turkey, and mayonnaise, so that the group has to make the sandwiches. These "personalizing" techniques go a long way toward humanizing a situation that for many people is the most overwhelming experience in their lives.

Information on hostage situations reveals that 80 percent of all people (police officers, hostages, criminals, and innocent bystanders) who die in hostage situations die when the authorities do not attempt negotiations and use force instead. This suggests that humanization works, even though it may take a great deal of time. Research also supports the conclusion that if hostages are not killed in the first thirty minutes of captivity, then the possibility of their being killed is drastically reduced. Captain Frank Bolz, Jr., the chief hostage negotiator for the New York Police Department, pointed out: "As more time passes, the likelihood that the perpetrator will harm you decreases. The bond that will form between both of you will be almost imperceptible at first. . . . As the ordeal lengthens, it will appear that it is you and he against the world outside."[65] After these critical thirty minutes of emotional instability, time works in favor of the hostages and the authorities. Initially, emotion is high and reason is low. But as time passes, these two factors level off.

This means, of course, that authorities should attempt to foster a relationship between criminal and hostage. The hostage's very life depends on the emotional state of the criminal; the longer the authorities can communicate with the criminal, the better. Moreover, the stress of holding captors grows very fatiguing for the hostage takers. The presence of Stockholm Syndrome works to the advantage of the hostage and the intermediary; when the third phase has occurred, violence and death are less likely.

The initial stress of a victim realizing that he has been kidnapped initiates the violent disruption of accepted norms, of the victim's reality framework. "How can this be happening to me?" is a common reaction. Whose reality framework includes the possibility of entering a bank to make a simple deposit or working at the bank and becoming a hostage? Who really considers that a vacation will turn into an indescribably traumatic number of hours or days spent in vulnerable captivity?

This initial shock has befallen all sorts of persons in extreme situations, and it soon gives way to the inexpressible horror of the first stage of captivity. Patty Hearst recalled that the first few days of her stay as a "People's Prisoner" were spent crying and feeling utterly helpless and scared. In Iran an entire year of stress preceded the actual capturing of the embassy in November of 1979. Still, none of the Americans were prepared for the maddening events of that day or the humiliation meted out by Iranian militants in the days to follow. This first phase of captivity is one of otherness, of something totally alien to the prisoner's previous existence. The old self begins to fall apart. Solzhenitsyn's remembrance of the labor camps, Des Pres's reports on Auschwitz, Bettelheim's account of the concentration camps—all views confirm the overwhelming nature of this initial phase of captivity.

This initial stage is one in which the captives are controlled, decisions are made for them and not by them, and where they exist as "kept" beings. Human beings are born into the world this way, and through captivity they return. Dependence becomes their regimen.

One writer described new captors as being up against "a total institution."[66] Total institutions—totalitarian societies, prisons, kidnapping scenarios, and so on—are invariably oppressive to individual interests. They are oppressive precisely because they result in the subject's forced infancy—in effect, his breakdown.

In the concentration camp this initial stage was referred to by the Gestapo as the "Prisoner's Welcome."[67] This welcome consisted of physical punishment, like whipping and kicking, and psychological punishments—prisoners were forced to curse their God, accuse themselves of vile actions, and accuse their wives of adultery and prostitution. According to reliable reports, this initiation continued for twelve hours and frequently lasted for twenty-four.

The purpose of the initiation was to break the resistance of the prisoners and to assure the prisoner of the guard's superiority. Such punishment results in a state of normlessness—of being thrown into a reality that represents a clean break with one's normal life. No wonder it has been called the hysteroid phase.[68]

In politics there is also a reality framework. For instance, the thought that the Soviet Union would unilaterally use the missiles it has amassed on the border of Western Europe seems beyond the borders of Petra Kelly's psyche. Consequently, when she hears the Soviet Union's propaganda claiming itself the great peacemaker, she believes the lies. Her reality framework demands that she does, just as the hostage's framework demands that he believes in his aggressor. Both adjust their reality frameworks to accommodate the aggressor.

In a hostage situation, 'positive' is defined primarily as the absence of negative. That is, if the hostages are not actually being beaten, then they react positively to their captors, forgetting or unconsciously ignoring the reality that the captors caused and maintain the entire negative environment in which the victims find themselves. This description by a victim of an airplane hijacking is a clear example of how the absence of negativity becomes positive in the eyes of captives:

After it was over and we were all safe I recognized that they had put me through hell, and had caused my parents and fiance a great deal of trauma. Yet, I was alive. I was alive because they had let me live. You know only a few people, if any, who hold your life in their hands and then give it back to you. After it was over and we were safe and they were in handcuffs, I walked over to them and kissed each one of them and said, "Thank you for giving me my life back."[69]

Another victim of the same hijacking expressed similar feelings: "They didn't have anything (the bombs turned out to be fake), but they were really great guys, I really want to go to their trial."[70] In the hostage syndrome the victim's need to survive outdistances his impulse to hate the person who has created his dilemma. His ego continues to function in pursuit of its primary goal—to keep the self alive.

Likewise, any negative action that the Soviets do not pursue, such as leaving the negotiation table or invading a country, becomes a positive contribution to the cause of peace in the mind of Europe.

There are many situations in which Stockholm Syndrome cannot develop. At the Hotel Tacloban there was too much bitterness on the part of the POWs to identify with the captors.[71] Valentine and other soldiers knew that the Japanese soldiers felt no remorse and that they would even giggle while their opponents writhed in agony and died. The sadism of the camps precluded any bonding between captor and captive.

Nor were U.S. captives in Iran ever in a position to develop Stockholm Syndrome. During interrogations in the first month of their captivity, the Americans were psychologically abused with threats and physically abused by being punched and kicked all over their bodies. Bill Beck, a communications officer in the assembly, reported how much he respected army medic Don Hohman for berating and generally disrespecting his oppressors. When they asked Hohman to eat without first untying his hands, he shouted: "Get away from me. Either I eat with my own hands or I won't eat at all."[72] He also rejected the Iranian food and told them to get some American food from the commissary. He lacked any respect for the militant students, and he insulted them with names like "ragheads," "horses' asses," "thieves," and "punks." This kind of perception makes sympathetic attribution nearly impossible.

Additionally, the extreme fear of captivity did not exist for many prisoners in Iran. Why? They knew that they were not going to be severely harmed; the Iranians were going to mete only so much violence before they stopped their abuse. Colonel Charles Scott figured that when he was dragged to the outer gates of the compound and exposed to the Iranian people, he was not going to be hit in the head. He knew this, for he could hear the guards yelling in Persian, "Don't hit them in the head, don't hit them in the head." The guards were making sure that no one put any permanent marks on him. This allowed Scott to say to himself, "Bear up to this; it's not going to get any worse."[73] It never did. In short, the captors felt like captives; they themselves were hostages of the U.S. government. They knew they would pay dearly if any of the Americans were critically hurt. Since the Americans' fear of death—a primary stress component of Stockholm Syndrome—was negated by the Iranians' fear, Stockholm Syndrome couldn't get a foothold.

At times it appeared that Stockholm Syndrome would develop. Marine Security Guard Sergeant William Quarles reported having been "touched" by one of the older guards. This guard told the story of how the SAVAK (the Shah's secret police) had killed his brother, sister, and father. The guard broke down in tears when he related how they were tortured. Quarles confessed to being greatly moved. However, at no time did the separate stages of Stockholm Syndrome appear.

When the U.S. hostages were finally released after 444 days in captivity in Iran, there was a great deal of anxiety in the United States as to whether the propaganda of the Iranian militants rubbed off on them. This fear was caused in part by released hostage Marine Corporal William Gallegos when he was interviewed by NBC. In the interview he expressed sympathy for the Iranian revolutionaries. This aroused the suspicion that the hostages may have been brainwashed. But again, the hostage syndrome is not brainwashing. According to Stanford University's Donald Lunde, a psychiatrist who has treated many kidnap victims, the hostages probably were not brainwashed: "I'd expect the hostages to have some quite positive feelings for their captors for the simple reason that these people have been playing a parental role with them and have kept them in a dependent state."[74] As a result, said Lunde, "they'll be making Anti-Shah, Anti-CIA statements for the first couple of weeks after their release."

Conditions for U.S. POWS in Hanoi were similarly unfit for the growth of hostage syndrome. POWs were kept in cells seven feet square; they were also segregated from one another. Communication was disallowed and punishable by solitary confinement.

In the concentration camps there were also very few seeds from which a bond could develop. Only rarely were guards kind to prisoners: Only a few SS refrained from making anti-Semitic remarks, hitting prisoners, killing them, and reporting them for punishment. For the most part the inmates were commodities—things to be used. When they no longer served any use, they were discarded. To accomplish this disposal, they were "processed" as in modern factory methods.

Survival is the goal of the various coping strategies I mentioned. Whether one survives depends largely on whether one can deal with the traumatization of being imprisoned. And whether a captive can handle this trauma depends, in turn, on whether he has had any previous experience with imprisonment and violence of the sort that extremity exposes him to. Most have not had any such experiences, and so the goal of captivity is to weather the initial shock of being a prisoner. For each day that hostages survive, they are thankful to all those forces beyond their control, one of which is the aggressor.

Each day it is possible for the people of Europe to look to the Soviet Union and thank them for not destroying the continent. In a psychological way, they do. Perhaps this is the reason one sees Europeans continually seeking to accommodate the Soviets, seeking a policy of friendly relations.

The drift of Europe toward neutralism or toward the Soviet Union represents a shift in identification of the hostage from his family and legitimate authorities in favor of his captor. The shift is unconscious on the part of Europe. The seemingly unrelated events, such as the decision to continue to assist the Soviet Union with the construction of the pipeline in spite of the Soviet involvement with Afghanistan, the refusal to join in sanction against Libya, and the protests against the deployment of U.S. missiles to offset the Soviet SS-20s all suggest that Europe is hostage to the Soviets.

Certainly the factors necessary to bring about hostage syndrome—the high level of stress, positive association with the Soviets—have all contributed to the bond that has formed between the Soviet Union and Europe.

In the following chapter I will explore the mechanisms of this identification, why it is unconscious, the reason it is so significant. In the last part of the book, I will attempt to show that the Soviets have, over the course of the past thirty years, actively and intentionally sought to create the situation by which Europe would become more dependent on the East and turn away from the West.

European reaction to the invasion of Afghanistan, the hijacking of the *Achille Lauro*, and the airport terrorism in Vienna and Rome demonstrates that the European drift away from the United States is reaching a dangerous point. Add to this the recent discovery that Greece's largest daily newspaper, *ETHNOS*, with a circulation of 180,000, was established with financing and support from the Soviet KGB for the purpose of spreading disinformation.[75]

The United States must act to counter this process. I will conclude with ways of reevaluating current U.S. policy so that the Soviet Union can be faced more successfully at the negotiating table and the European drift toward the Soviets can be arrested.

# 3

# *Identification*

The fundamental dynamic of the Stockholm Syndrome that distinguishes it from other methods of psychological adaptations to stressful situations is the identification bond that forms between hostages and captors. It is also different from the previously mentioned defenses against extremity in that it is an unconscious mechanism. During a hostage crisis, this bond of identification develops, causing the hostages to attempt to defend their captors physically, emotionally, and ideologically against all external agencies and authorities. This defense of the captors occurs with no apparent regard for logic or reason.

That the captors hold the hostages in a state of constant danger seems to make no impression on the hostages. Identification with their captors causes the hostages to internalize sympathies for them and create justifications for their actions, just as children do for their parents. Like a child's bond with his parents, the hostage's bond of identification with his captor continues long after the immediate crisis has been resolved and the hostage is no longer vulnerable to his captor.

The sympathies that some hostages develop during a hostage crisis are not motivated by an immediate and conscious strategy for survival. If that were the case, except for some residual effects of the stress caused by the hostage situation, we would expect a fairly rapid development of some strongly negative feelings on the part of the hostage toward his captor after the episode. Instead, we see continued sympathy. Some hostages have trouble understanding why they feel the sympathy that they do, but they continue to feel it.

The duration of these feelings and the bond of identification is highly variable from individual to individual and from case to case. The duration of the bond depends on several factors external to the hostages themselves, such as the length of their captivity, as well as the intensity of the positive contacts between them and their captors.

The identification bond that forms between hostage and captor is so significant and pervasive because it closely parallels the identification process that occurs between child and parent. The degree to which it parallels and mirrors that process suggests why its effects are so compelling.

Young children regard the authority of adults as very great. The child's admiration of adults, beginning approximately at the age of three, tends to overrule the conflict between them, a conflict born of adult constraints and authority. The clinical psychologist David Shapiro described this stage of development so perceptively:

> [Moral] judgment begins with the child's literal acceptance of the moral authority of adult constraints and the reification of these into absolute law: wrong is what is prohibited and punishable by adults. . . . The moral imperatives of adult authority become in this gradual way internalized. . . . The child's aim in emulating adults is to close the gap [between them], but [the child] cannot in actual fact become what he's not. In this sense, the process of identification can never be completely successful. As the normal child grows, experiencing his own autonomy and significance, his interest in emulating adults diminishes.[1]

What is most striking about the moral development of children, from a stage of adherence to adult authority to a growth into personal autonomy, is that this is only the norm. The very experience of being a captive puts many adults right back into a state of childhood obedience, a state in which the commands of authority are most strongly felt. This response to extreme situations is known as "traumatic infantilism."[2]

After the 1977 siege of the B'nai B'rith office in Washington, D.C., by a group of Hanafi Muslims, and during the captivity of Americans by Iranian radicals in Teheran, psychiatrists and psychologists reviewed and built upon the large body of material available on how individuals adapt to radically new and violent situations and on the psychological makeup of hostages.

The conclusions reached by the various experts working in the field were not always in agreement, but there was a definite agreement on certain key points. Primarily, the point that emerged was that persons, when confronted with a suddenly hostile environment, respond with the early adaptive behavior of childhood.

Traumatic infantilism accounts for the obedience—the compliant and submissive behavior—witnessed in many individuals in a hostage situation. Psychiatrists pointed out that a hostage's utter dependence on his captors for everything—from food to permission to go to the bathroom—was a primary cause of Stockholm Syndrome. In short, "the dependent" sees the captor as the only source of the life and limited freedom he has.[3]

According to this scheme, the Stockholm Syndrome can be broken into two main segments. The event of being taken hostage—the experience of having criminals or terrorists invade one's home or one's vehicle of travel and making outrageous demands—destroys the support system and reality framework that each individual relies on. The second period is the entire period of being held captive.

During the first segment, law and justice, not to mention social conventions and ideas of fairness, become almost instantly irrelevant, and the workings of fate take the place of order and predictability. Psychologists call this a state of "deregularity" or "normlessness."[4] It is as if, at that moment, the sky really did fall. This experience violently thrusts the individual into a psychologically regressive process. Once the process has been set in motion, the hostage will develop an attachment and then an identification to the stronger, authoritarian figure, his captor. This parallels the identification he developed as a child with his parents.

Traumatic infantilism renders impotent the assumptions and sophistication of adulthood, forcing the captive into a position of absolute vulnerability and need of that authoritarian figure.[5] The oppressor's objective at this first stage is often to traumatize prisoners. The result is a regression to childlike behavior colored by short-term thinking, the inability to focus on any long-term objectives, irrationality, and wishful thinking. The captive also tends to deny anything that is unpleasant.

Captivity creates strong feelings in a group when survival is the chief concern. The group is held together by a common danger that is transferred to a common enemy: the outgroup. A strong interdependence between captors and captives grows out of a common goal: survival. They begin as opponents, but they turn into partners—"covictims"—and raise their backs against the common enemy that threatens them. A "we" feeling is established. Part of the identification between captives and captors may be erotic; captives may be attracted to the brute simplicity of this new "caveman," captor, who is free of the rules of civil conduct and might be a feared but desired fantasy.[6]

After much exposure to domineering, sadistic control, the victims may assume the characteristics of the aggressors. Some prisoners carry some of the character of the aggressor with them after they have been liberated.

Sigmund Freud suggested that the identification by the son to his father is the result of the resolution of the Oedipal complex.

> This type of identification is one in which a person identifies with the probabilities laid down by an authority figure. The purpose of this kind of identification is to enable one to avoid punishment by being obedient to the demands of the potential enemy. One identifies out of fear rather than love. Such identifications are the foundations upon which the conscience is based. . . . As the child grows older, similar identifications are made with the demands of other dominant people.[7]

The Freudian concept depends primarily on identification as a way of avoiding punishment. In this context avoiding punishment can also be understood as a means of gaining affection. Identification with an authority might also be seen as the child's way of eliminating the conflict between his own desire for autonomy and the authority's tendency to restrain him.

According to Freud's view, the process of identification represents a resolution of the Oedipal complex. Briefly, the Oedipal complex is the desire by a son to possess his mother. In such a scenario, the son perceives the father, who also competes for the mother's affection, as the enemy. The father stands between the son and his object. Eventually, the son must come to realize that he cannot defeat the stronger, more dominant father, and so he identifies with his father and successfully controls his desire.

By this resolution, the son avoids the "punishment" of the constant state of defeat he feels at the hands of his dominant father. Other psychologists have drawn comparable conclusions, saying that the goal of a child's identification with an authority is to erase conflict with that authority. In this way identification closes the gap between the child and the adult. This represents in Freud's view the beginning of a new sense of self.

In Freud's understanding of the human psyche, there are three competing interests, usually held in balance: the id, which represents the desire, the libido; the superego, which represents the conscience; and the ego, which mediates between the id and the superego, maintaining a balance between the id's desire to possess the mother and the superego's sense of guilt and fear.

The mechanism that Freud described is relevant to the hostage syndrome. After the initial trauma, the individual is thrust back to a psychological childhood in which he is vulnerable to and dominated by stronger, authoritarian figures. The hostage desires to be free, but his desire, just like a young boy's desire for his mother, is thwarted by the existence of a dominant figure. Like the young boy, the hostage resolves the crisis by identification with his captor to ensure the survival of his psyche and to avoid punishment.

Anna Freud cited analogous cases of two children who practiced identification to avoid being overwhelmed by anxiety. One, an elementary school boy, used to make faces at his teacher, who frequently scolded him. These faces would cause the entire class to burst out laughing, and so the boy was reprimanded. When the boy, his master, and a psychologist were together, the situation was explained: The boy's faces were caricatures of the angry expressions of the teacher. The boy identified himself with the teacher's anger and copied his expression as he spoke. Through his grimaces he was likening himself to or identifying himself with a dreaded external object.[8]

Another little girl was afraid of crossing the hall in the dark because she feared ghosts. But she managed a way of crossing the hall that would minimize her anxiety: She would run across the hall, making all sorts of unusual gestures as she went. She explained to her brother how she overcame her fear: "There is no need to be afraid in the hall, you just have to pretend that you're the ghost who might meet you." Her gestures represented the movements that she figured ghosts would make. Like the schoolboy, she deflected some of her fear by becoming like her aggressor.

A further implication of these episodes was revealed by Anna Freud:

If the doctor looks down a child's throat or carries out some small operation, we may be quite sure that these frightening experiences will be the subject of the next game; but we must not in that connection overlook the fact that there is a yield of pleasure from another source. As the child passes from the passivity of the experience to the activity of the game, he hands on the disagreeable experience to one of his playmates and in this way revenges himself on a substitute.[9]

There are quite a few children's games in which a dreaded object is turned into an object of pleasurable security.

Through identification with their aggressors, children and hostages merge their identities with and strive to become like the individuals whose power they must fear. Anna Freud said, "By impersonating the aggressor, assuming his attributes or imitating his aggression, the child transforms himself from the person threatened into the person who makes the threat.''[10] Thus, the authority of adults, teachers, and authorities in general is diminished by the child's or hostage's transformation from a passive recipient of commands and rules to an active participation in the threat. By understanding the behavior of aggressors, the hostage/child seeks to turn them into allies. By identifying, one seeks to deal with the surrounding horror by acting. Identification is an active adaptation to extremity, which keeps the ego from being overwhelmed by realistic worries.

Even in Nazi concentration camps, there were instances in which the inmates imitated their guards. Some older prisoners went beyond merely imitating their behavior; they also took on the attitudes of the Gestapo, especially their attitudes toward the unfit prisoners. How much older prisoners assimilated Gestapo attitudes can be seen in the way they killed other prisoners. Killing unfit prisoners was a means of self-protection for the older prisoners, because unfit prisoners were weak and could be a liability to the whole labor gang to which they belonged. But the way in which the older prisoners tortured them for several days and slowly killed them was borrowed from the Gestapo.[11]

Identification did not stop at aggressive behavior. Prisoners tried to claim old pieces of Gestapo uniforms. When this was not possible, they tried to remodel their own uniforms to resemble those of the Gestapo. They continued this even though they were punished for it. When asked why they continued, they replied that they wanted to look like the guards.

Prisoners prided themselves on being as tough as Gestapo members. Prisoners even went so far as to copy Gestapo leisure activities. One of the games the guards played was to find out who could be hit the longest without complaining. This game was imitated by older prisoners, even though they were already hit enough in their daily activities.

The prisoners also took part in enforcing useless rules—like having prisoners wash the inside of their shoes or having them stand at perfect attention—simply because these rules were once used by the guards.

Most psychologists agree that the period of identification occurs around the age of five years, about the time when the Oedipal complex is resolved in the normal child. Most experts believe that the experience of being held hostage places one psychologically at about the age of five years.

An individual will try to anticipate the desires of the person he has identified with. This might suggest a reason not just for the affections a hostage feels for his captor long after the event has been concluded, but also a reason why a former hostage will continue to make efforts to protect his captor. Patricia Hearst did this at her trial by trying to protect the Harrises.

By carefully observing the captor, a hostage learns how to behave to best protect his life and to earn rewards, such as being allowed to go to the bathroom or having a blindfold loosened. This learned behavior will always involve and become identification with the captor.

What occurs during identification is a generalization on the part of the child, and therefore on the part of the hostage. He begins to anticipate what is acceptable and correct.

By assimilating wholly the behavior of the captor, the hostage is forced to "lose" the character that he has had through his life. The traumatic experience overturns his character, and the apparent inability of authorities to effect his release forces the hostage back to a "start-over" point where he must begin again and learn to be an individual.

The views of Jean Piaget, expert on child development, can explain how a hostage's moral structure can break down so easily.[12] Piaget concerned himself primarily with the stages of growth in the child, which correspond with the child's development in his ability to understand the external world. In this context, moral development was a focus of his examination.

A child's morality is not chosen nor arrived at by rational means. Piaget said:

The first moral precept of the child is obedience and the first criterion of what is good is, for a long time, the will of the parents. At this first stage a child goes by a "heteronomous morality." Literally, this means his morality is produced by authorities or things external to him. Children at this first stage—three to six years old—are moral "absolutists." They believe that rules are fixed, absolute and unchangeable.[13]

This is not only true for the rules that parents give but for the rules of games as well. If the rule is broken, a child feels that punishment inevitably and quickly follows—from parents, teachers, or even God. The child's earliest moral judgments place him in a stage of "moral realism": What is right is to obey the will of an adult; what is wrong is to obey a will of one's own.

A normal child evolves from a stage of submission to adults to a position of equality with them. A hostage gets stuck in the first stage of child morality; he remains fixed by the captor's demands and rules.

In this respect the hostage resembles a child at a moral realist stage—a child of three to six years old.

Neither children nor hostages account for the motives of the aggressor. Appraising moral motives occurs at a later stage of child development, usually around the age of ten. Morality at the earliest stage concerns the "damage that is done" by a person. One's guilt is determined solely by the amount of damage one has caused.

A classic experiment by Piaget involved the notion of intention. A young child, when asked to decide whether it was worse to break two glasses while doing something that is permitted or to break a single glass while doing something naughty, will always say that the situation in which the two glasses were broken was the worst. According to Piaget—and another respected expert, Lawrence Kohlberg—moral judgment emerges in steps. Younger children adopt an objective point of view, because a literal interest in the amount of damage wrought reflects their overall conception of behaviors and consequences. The first stage Kohlberg labeled the "punishment and obedience orientation." This stage is clearly evident in the child's literal obedience to rules and authority. Dependents learn to think like the authority and confuse the authority's perspective with their own.

Older children have a subjective orientation. That is, they would identify the situation in which the rules were broken as being the worst only if the intention to break the rules was itself immoral. This stage of morality Piaget called "autonomous morality" or the morality of reciprocity.

If children hear a story about a child who purposefully pushes another child off the monkey bars at school, the older children think this is naughty, even if the pusher intends only a little harm; younger children feel that intending a small hurt is less serious than causing an unintended big hurt.

Hostages, like children at the earliest stage of their moral development, look primarily at the consequences of a deed, its external aspect. They may overlook the motive for an action, its internal aspect. This may also hold a clue as to why hostages defend their captors against all external agencies. The hostage perceives the damage wrought by the captor as minimal—and positive—if everyone stays alive.

Of the views presented here, none provides an exact explanation for the process of identification or why the bond forms. But taken together, a pattern emerges that allows us to make some parallels between individual hostages and Europe.

In the following pages I will attempt to show how these psychological insights shed light on the current situation in Europe. Europeans are identifying with the enemy. But first it is important to remember that identification is a means by which the hostage avoids punishment. In Europe, this punishment is perceived as the use of Soviet military might against the continent. Remember that moral judgment is suspended in the hostage, who returns to a childlike obedience. This suggests an explanation as to why hostage Europe drifts in the direction of the East.

Just as during severe family crises a child might seek out a strong authority figure from whom to gain support, Europe is leaning to the Soviet Union for that support. The cruel irony is that it is the Soviet Union that has created the crisis.

In historical terms, the unification of Europe is very recent. We can almost say it is in its infancy as a unified continent, yet signs of its disunity are everywhere.

The child's—and the hostage's—morality of obedience evolves to a stage where cooperation replaces submission. Mutual respect follows from this cooperation. The parallel with Stockholm Syndrome is clear: The third phase in the hostage–captor relationship occurs when the captor reciprocates the captive's understanding. Signs of this mutuality are present between Europe and the Soviet Union. "In identification," Freud wrote, "one ego comes to resemble another one."[14] Identification promotes likenesses and therefore safety.

In the next chapter, I will try to merge both roads of my argument—the analogy that likens Europe to a captor in a hostage crisis.

# 4

# *The European Alliance*

Prior to World War II, Europe was a federation of nations and states at odds. The reality that emerged after World War II demanded that the strife and bitterness of the past be forgotten and a new way of coexistence be created.

New geographical realities emerged after the war that determined the United States' willingness to assist the European reconstruction. As former Undersecretary of State George Ball said: "We have felt the increasing weight of the burdens and responsibilities of leadership—increased geometrically by the existence of a real and present danger from communist ambitions—we have wished, sometimes wistfully, for a closer and stronger Atlantic partnership."[1] Implied in Ball's statement was the danger posed by the Soviet Union to the future of a free and democratic Europe.

By late 1945 Western Europe sensed the threat from the East. Eastern Europe was nearly under Soviet rule, and both U.S. and European statesmen feared the Soviet's further expansion. Because of the power vacuum left by the defeat of Germany and Japan, Stalin had made his move against Western Europe and East Asia. Naturally, fear of another war in Europe ran very high. This fear was compounded by Europe's weakness due to crippling economic problems, problems that the United States helped to alleviate with the Marshall Plan.

Though this economic program was to be eminently successful, Europeans wanted and needed more. In his famous iron curtain speech, Churchill reminded the world that "the Soviet Union was an 'expanionist state.'" He warned that an alliance of the English-speaking peoples was the prerequisite for U.S. and British security and world peace. At the same time, the U.S. Foreign Service's foremost expert on the Soviet Union, George Kennan, argued that the United States' "preparedness" to use biological and atomic weapons was essential, because "the mere fact of such preparedness may be the only deterrent to Russian aggressive actions and in this sense the only sure guarantee of peace."[2] Zbigniew Brzezinski, national security adviser to President Carter, could justify U.S. involvement in Europe by the Soviets' historical record of "unremitting expansionism." In postwar Europe, therefore, one of the crucial components for Stockholm Syndrome was already in place: Europe was a continent in a state of fear.

The North Atlantic Treaty was effected on April 4, 1949. This treaty was a promise that an attack on even one of the members of NATO—Belgium, Canada, Denmark, France, Great Britain, Iceland, Italy, Luxembourg, the Netherlands, Norway, Portugal, or the United States—would count as an attack on all of them. The great importance of this commitment was made plain to the allied nations, especially after the Soviet's conquest of Czechoslovakia early in 1948.

On March 17, 1948, Truman spoke to Congress, addressing this problem: "The tragic death of the Republic of Czechoslovakia has sent a shock wave throughout the civilized world."[3] Less than three months later, the Senate overwhelmingly passed the Vandenberg resolution, calling for the United States to provide a "collective security arrangement" in Europe. To George Kennan, this arrangement was a "modest security shield" for a recovering Europe. It also served as a muscle-flexing signal to Moscow; the United States would count any threat to Europe as a threat to its own interests.

Two developments that had occurred by 1948 made the Soviets take notice. One was the discussion within the U.S. government about placing B-52 bombers, the carriers of the atomic bomb, to bases in Europe within striking distance of the Soviet Union. The other was the Marshall Plan itself, which Stalin interpreted as a military commitment to rebuild and eventually rearm Germany. These moves led Stalin to believe only the worst about the United States' intentions.

George Kennan's policy of "containment," which called for "the containment of Russian expansive tendencies to be carried out by military action," was put into effect. Kennan cautioned: "We must make the Russians understand that they must confine their security demands to our security demands. . . . Communist ideology, has taught the Soviets that the outside world is hostile."[4]

It was the Soviet Union's duty to eventually overthrow the political forces beyond their borders. Kennan was not alone in this opinion. Georges Bidault, who had worked with communists in the resistance and had run the French Foreign Ministry since the end of 1944, believed "the goal of Communism was to eradicate Western civilization."

French leader de Gaulle had also changed his tune: "We are occidentals, loyal supporters of a particular view of man, of life, of law and international relations."[5] Only three years earlier he had proposed an alliance with Stalin, but he then became increasingly anticommunist.

In his book *NATO in Transition*, Timothy Stanley explained the key to the Soviet Union's strategic policy concerning Europe: Divide the alliance. The method the Soviets have chosen to accomplish that aim is psychological—make Europe hostage, lead Europe to identify with the East, and the alliance will end.

Western Europe felt the menace of a Soviet invasion immediately after the war. In 1949 it recognized Soviet nuclear capability. The alliance received another shock and indication of the strength of the Soviet Union on June 25, 1950, when North Korean forces crossed the thirty-eighth parallel. It was the first time a communist state had engaged in overt military aggression. In the following months intelligence reports were able to prove conclusively that it represented careful planning and a deliberate policy choice that had been approved, if not dictated, in the Kremlin. These events laid the groundwork for the militarization of the U.S. attitude toward the Soviets that has been the dominant feature of U.S. policy ever since.

Like a child before an authoritarian father, Europe was put on notice. Europe had to consider the ominous possibility that other sites of aggression might be considered by the Soviets—sites that could include Europe.

The Soviet Union, from the beginning an ominous presence for Europe, became an overtly threatening one. Europe found itself having to respond to the Soviet Union's military potential. This reaction created the heightened stress and tension felt around the world but most pointedly in Europe during the cold war years.

As we will see, however, it was the conclusion of the cold war years that brought the tension in Europe to greater heights, heights that could trigger the beginning of the hostage syndrome.

After the Korean War the Europeans were hardly satisfied with a mere declaration of intent from the United States. Europe wanted tangible evidence that the United States would live up to its promise, and the United States was only too glad to fulfill this request. General Dwight D. Eisenhower was appointed NATO's first supreme commander. U.S. military doctrine, not very popular among NATO countries, gave up the idea of a conventional war and switched to the idea of a nuclear war or nothing. The idea was to use "massive retaliation" against any Soviet strike—in effect, a swift and devastating use of nuclear weapons. This military stance implied that Europe would not be defended on the ground or at least would not participate in its own defense.

By the end of the 1950s the dilemma was clear but dark: the next war could not be a nuclear war—for this could lead to global incineration—and could not be a conventional war. The alternatives showed no escape.

The way out was "deterrence." The ultimate weapon would not—could not—be used to fight a war. But it could be used to stop one. By 1956 President Eisenhower entered in his diary what many U.S. officials already knew: "It was calculated (in the event of a nuclear war) that something on the order of 65% of the population would require medical care of some kind and in most instances no opportunity whatever to get it."[6] Despite the United States' military superiority at the time, the president believed that in a war the United States would suffer a total economic collapse. Nuclear war—unlike other wars—could not be fought. In Khrushchev's words, if it were fought, "the survivors would envy the dead."

Hence the strategies of deterrence and "flexible response" were employed, and these remain cornerstones of U.S. nuclear policy. Despite U.S. and allied attacks on these plans, they may well be the best for promoting security in the United States and Europe. The burden of proof rests on the shoulders of opinion makers and statesmen who attack deterrence as a method of guarding against war. Deterrence has a track record.

This was the presumption behind Harry Truman's verdict that the United States would hold the atomic weapon as a "trustee" for civilization. Jean Monet, the secretary general of the League of Nations, enthusiastically backed the military policy of deterrence. After returning from the United States in 1949, he concluded: "America is on the move but it is neither reactionary nor imperialist. It does not want war, but it will go to war if need be. A great change has occurred there recently: preparation to make war has given way to preparation to prevent it."[7]

It was Monet who originated the slogan, "America will be the great arsenal of democracy." He was an integrationist and believed that a federation of the West, including Britain, would enable Europe to solve its problems and prevent war. Monet was an avid supporter of NATO, and NATO did indeed seem to be working.

With the recovery program under way and the U.S. military commitment and policy of deterrence in place, it seemed that the alliance was secure. From a financial perspective the $13 billion spent by the United States on Europe between 1948 and 1952 transformed the political economy of the continent. By 1951 the "dollar gap" had been greatly narrowed. Exports from the United States went up sharply, and contrary to the prediction of the communists, imports from the United States were down. In four years industrial production in France rose 32 percent and in Italy and in the Netherlands, 56 percent. With this staggering success it is difficult now to see how anything could have been wrong between the United States and its "first line of defense"—the NATO countries. But changing times and events—like the Soviet development of nuclear weapons—led to different ideas about the purpose of NATO and the duties of the partners in the alliance. These changing realities caused opposing opinions, disappointments, and even disgust. In turn, these contrary views led to rifts in the alliance that laid the foundation for European accommodation with the Soviets and Stockholm Syndrome.

Even at the onset of the European recovery program the U.S. ambassador to London reported that "anti-American sentiment in Europe bordered on the pathological." England's weakness and dependence, he continued, "were a bitter pill to a country accustomed to full control of her natural destiny."[8]

A candid parody that made its way around London pubs captured the popular feeling in Great Britain:

Our uncle which art in America
Sam be thy name
Thy navy come, thy will be done
In London as 'tis in Washington
Give us this day our Marshall aid
And forgive us our un-American activities,
As we forgive your American activities against us;
And lead us not into socialism
But deliver us from communism
For thine is our kingdom
The atom power and the tory
Forever and ever: G-men[9]

Though the Marshall Plan supplied Britain with 66 percent of its bread ration, 60 percent of its oil, and 20 percent of the country's coal requirements, it produced mixed reactions. Receiving so much produced more than a little humility in the Europeans. They also realized that cooperation was owed in return.

It was in this spirit that de Gaulle later explained in his *Memoirs* that "NATO was the price Americans had exacted for the Marshall Plan."[10] He meant, of course, that while the U.S. guarantee to defend Europe was still an insurance policy, NATO remained under the authority of the United States. Membership in NATO limited the freedom of members to pursue their own policies. The United States' NATO plan would, he believed, lead inevitably to an "American Europe," a Europe incapable by its very nature of having its own defense or foreign policy and always subject to U.S. wishes.

By 1958 he had begun his campaign to remove the United States' hold on Europe. In March 1959 he withdrew the French Mediterranean fleet from the NATO command. He also put a ban on U.S. atomic weapons in France while he increased efforts to produce his own. Since the Soviet Union had already tested a devastating hydrogen bomb in 1953, de Gaulle lost confidence in the U.S. nuclear umbrella. Now a war between the Soviet Union and the United States might end in U.S. defeat and leave Europe alone and defenseless. Another possibility was a Soviet conventional attack on Europe or even a quick nuclear strike, which, due to Soviet capabilities, the United States would be hesitant to counter. Many possibilities seemed to point toward the next major war being fought in Europe.

Aside from the military issue, de Gaulle had come to regard NATO as just a U.S. appendage, which he found demeaning to France. His goal was a "European Europe," as opposed to a client Europe. This "new Europe" was to include the Soviet Union but exclude the United States. By 1966 de Gaulle announced the French intention to withdraw from the military organization of NATO but not from NATO itself, thereby keeping a foot in the security door. He made plans to ensure a Franco–Soviet détente. Again, de Gaulle felt impelled to do this by the force of changing events: France could be destroyed, he said in a famous statement in 1963, unless "the aggressor is deterred from the attempt by the certainty that he too will suffer frightful destruction." Yet while he questioned the dependability of the United States' nuclear deterrent, he did not wish to give it up.

The issue of military might has always nagged at the alliance. The stationing of U.S. nuclear weapons in Europe has always been a volatile subject, causing discord. While U.S. statesmen and opinion makers expressed great confidence in the idea of deterrence, countries like Germany questioned the need for recruiting their own troops, since NATO was planning to use atomic weapons in a war, and these would destroy Germany, troops, civilians, and all. In public opinion polls the German population overwhelmingly rejected the idea of being defended with nuclear weapons.

Also troublesome to the alliance are rights concerning the character and use of the weapons. In 1952, Marshall Juin, the French general in charge of NATO's ground troops, was prohibited from knowing the number and character of atomic arms with which his troops might be equipped. It has been that way ever since. Legal control and the decision to use such weapons has remained with the United States to this day. The 1952 Forces Convention Pact gives the United States a free hand to deploy on German territory whatever weapons and forces it deems necessary. And the convention contains no restrictions on the development of nuclear weapons.[11]

Reluctance to accept these deadly weapons prevailed, even while they were being deployed and developed. The British exploded their first hydrogen bomb on Christmas in May 1958. Randolph Churchill taunted the U.S. chamber of commerce in London: "Britain can now down 12 cities in the region of Stalingrad and Moscow from bases in Cyprus. We are once again a great power."[12] This gentle gallows humor belied the real situation in England and on the continent.

The British decision to develop a nuclear deterrent only came after a great deal of heated debate on both moral and practical grounds in opposition to the bomb. It was fear, and the uncertainty of just what would happen if a nuclear confrontation took place, that fueled these bitter exchanges. By the late 1950s the Campaign for Nuclear Disarmament was organizing mass marches to demand unilateral British nuclear disarmament. Even in the military establishment many felt it made no sense for Britain to put limited resources into H-bombs and missiles.

Concerns over nuclear might are not the only troubles that have threatened the alliance. Familiar changes like "rough parity" between the United States and the Soviet Union, and the authority lost by the United States in Vietnam, Watergate, and Iran couldn't help but hurt the Atlantic partnership.

Differing opinions about Vietnam caused great strains in the alliance. *The Wall Street Journal* reported in May 1967 that 80 percent of the West European public was against what the United States was doing in Vietnam.[13] The writer of the article commented, "The typical European wants the United States to quit fighting and clear out." To Europeans, the war was not only immoral but futile. By 1968 the protest movement was international and had a disruptive effect on the alliance. U.S. credibility in Europe suffered greatly.

To this day, however, the sharpest wedge in the alliance concerns the conduct of military operations affecting Europe. A number of irksome issues end up leading to disagreements. Should there be nuclear weapons in Europe? If so, what kind and how many? Should the United States pursue a military policy designed to accommodate the Soviets, or should rearmaments be the first order of business? Should the allies obey when the United States asks for sanctions to punish the Soviet Union and other nations for military adventurism or terrorism? Should the United States carry on with the Soviets as if the 1970s framework of détente had never ended? Must the United States avoid confrontation with the Soviets, even when international opinion finds the Soviets to be wrong? Must arms control talks and other confidence-building measures be pursued for the sake of appearances, even if substantive progress looks hopeless? Is any posture toward the Soviets, except a repeat of the 1950s cold war, permissible?

The caution relayed in these questions is born of fear. Since the ominous mushroom cloud rose above Hiroshima more than forty years ago, humankind has known the unspeakable power and horror of atomic weapons. Fear, of course, is more than justified. The picture of what a nuclear strike would look like has been sketched by responsible scientists and medical experts.

Imagine a nuclear explosion over New York, London, Paris, or Munich, such as what Jonathan Schell has frightened us with in his book *The Fate of the Earth*.[14] The dropping of a one-megaton bomb, bearing approximately sixty times the explosive force of the one dropped on Hiroshima, would produce inconceivable horror. Such a bomb exploding about a mile and a half above the Empire State Building would devastate every building between Battery Park and 125th Street, every structure within a radius of four miles. It would be devastating to buildings between the Northern end of Staten Island and the George Washington Bridge—an area of 500 square miles. Persons and debris would be treated the same; both would be blown away by the shock wave. Within a radius of 100 square miles, walls, roofs and ceilings will tumble if they have not already been destroyed.[15] People and furniture will be hurled into the streets. At ground level, the shock wave will send broken panes of glass and other

sharp-edged objects through the air at high velocities, inevitably causing death and serious injuries to those in the waves. Since debris—and
people—inside buildings will be blasted to the streets, people outside
will be buried alive in debris.

The resulting windstorm will reach a velocity of 400 miles per hour
to almost two miles above the earth, and it will be as high as 180 miles
per hour at a distance of three and a half miles away. The fireball
caused by the explosion will in a short time reach a distance of a mile
and will have risen six miles in the air. The town below will be exposed to its heat for about ten seconds. People outside at the time of
the explosion will probably die of third-degree burns within a radius of
about nine miles. Those near to the center of the explosion will be
burned up on the spot. From Greenwich village to Central Park in
New York City, the heat will be so intense that metal and glass will
just melt. Everything inflammable within a radius of nine miles will
burst into flames, so that a total of 420 square miles will be exposed to
fire. The fireball will emit a glaring white light for about thirty
seconds. Simultaneously, the incredible heat will torch everything that
is inflammable and melt windows, cars, lamp posts--in short,
anything made of metal or glass. People, whether in the street or in
buildings, will catch fire and burn beyond recognition in seconds. The
kind of death at Hiroshima will be repeated. Instead of 100,000 people, however, several million will be affected.

The city and its people will be transformed into a smoldering heap
of rubble. There may be a few survivors in areas peripheral to the
center of the explosion, but the ensuing fire will force them to abandon their relatives and others unable to flee, or to perish with them.

Incredibly, this would just be the tip of the iceberg. We are speaking of just one megaton bomb. The nuclear superpowers currently
possess about 120 nuclear weapons of five, nine, fifteen, and twenty
megatons. NATO and the Soviet Union have more than 15,000
nuclear warheads designed solely for use in European countries. If a
one-megaton bomb were dropped into a city like New York or
Detroit, the United States would lose more people than it lost in all of
World War II.

Add to these short-term consequences the long-term effects of
sparse medical attention, ruined hospitals, no electricity and communication systems, and the scenario resembles an eternal nightmare.
The water supply and the atmosphere itself would be poisoned, as
would every variety of food. Such scientists as Carl Sagan predict the
net result would be a "nuclear winter," since radioactive materials

and other particles from the explosion would keep out the sun's rays. All of humanity would be threatened, for scientists maintain that the globe would be too contaminated for life to continue. But since the situation has not been witnessed, it is impossible to describe just how extensive the damage would be.

Nuclear weapons inspire unparalleled dread and loathing. It is common knowledge that they should not be used, not in a "limited" war and certainly not in an all-out "spasm" war. No one can say for sure how a nation would respond if it were attacked, and no one wants to find out. In this case, it is best that the unknown be left unknown. To paraphrase Winston Churchill, there are enough weapons now to make the rubble bounce. Seventy times enough.[16] As Joseph Nye wrote, we are the first generation since Genesis with the capacity to destroy God's creation.[17]

Although this fear is healthy, it cannot form the foundation for a nuclear policy. If fear were the only component of U.S. and NATO military policy, nuclear weapons would not only be reduced but done away with altogether. The dangers of "unilateral disarmament" or "abolition" should be obvious, but some "advisers" recommend that we try these suicidal policies.

The dangers of thinking through fear in making military policy were stated convincingly by Professor Richard Pipes, a former member of the National Security Council, in his book *Survival is Not Enough*: "Fear of nuclear weapons especially in its overt and hysterical forms, does not contribute to peace; on the contrary, it serves to encourage those in the Soviet Union who want to use them to terrorize and blackmail foreign powers and their citizens."[18] It is not clear thinking but fear that so often leads NATO countries to accommodate Soviet wishes. Fear opens the door to intimidation, and intimidation tills the soil for the appearance of stress and hostage syndrome.

Everywhere we find opinion makers, journalists, generals, scientists, moral philosophers, and psychologists recommending that we address the issue while looking through the prison bars of fright. In such books as *Thinking About the Next War* by New York journalist Thomas Powers[19]; *Generals for Peace and Disarmament* written by former generals and ambassadors from eight NATO countries[20]; George Kennan's *The Nuclear Delusion*[21] and an anthology, *The Nuclear Crisis Reader*,[22] by renowned intellectuals in several disciplines, the reader is fed a smorgasbord of questionable logic and urgent policy directives, all warmed by fear. The kind of fear presented serves to wipe out the rationality required to make sound decisions. A look at some of the conclusions drawn by those who are supposed to be the best informed suggests that nuclear anxiety—not clear thinking—is really pulling the strings.

In Power's book we learn that "either we get rid of nuclear weapons or we'll experience a holocaust." This either/or advice obviously ignores any third or even fourth alternative. History since World War II has shown that although wars are now fought outside of Europe, accounting for the death of 25 million persons, no one has tested NATO's nuclear resolve in Europe. This is true despite the hills and valleys the superpowers have traveled over—known as cold wars and "thaws"—for some forty years.

Powers also states, "History shows that war occurs 6.2 times every decade." What this statistic doesn't show is the frequency of war between nuclear powers. More importantly, it does not support Powers's overarching conclusion that we should do away with all nuclear weapons.

Powers also turns our heads with the paradoxical conclusion that "the more prepared we are for a nuclear war, the worse it will be." Yes, the war will be worse in the sense that if we and the Soviets have 10,000 warheads each, instead of 5,000, the destructive power, or "payload," will be greater. But the argument is deceptive in two ways. For one, whether the confrontation is fought with 2,000 warheads or 10,000 will make no difference in the United States or the Soviet Union; either figure is a recipe for total destruction. On the other hand, being more prepared may prevent our being attacked in the first place. Believers in deterrence tell us this is the justification for having an "overkill" capacity. So Powers's statement might be amended to read, "The greater advantage one side amasses, the greater the likelihood of a war." This makes more sense to me.[23]

NATO generals recommend policies that are short on logic and downright dangerous. Lord Mountbatten is quoted as saying, "Nuclear weapons serve no military purpose." Kennan has also taken this position. Their sweeping generalizations, if put into practice, would not only sweep away the fears of the generals, but their security too. Isn't defense a "military purpose"? Although the weapons may not serve an offensive purpose, they do deter attacks.

After enlisting Mountbatten as an authority on nuclear weaponry, the generals asserted that "it is deplorable for religious institutions not to take a strong stance on nuclear weapons. [This is so] because, as the American Catholic bishops pointed out in their Pastoral Letter, nuclear war threatens the existence of the planet."[24] For the life of me

I cannot grasp this conclusion. Perhaps it should be taken on faith. Why does it contradict religious values to defend one's country? Would it be acceptable for religious institutions to support unilateral nuclear disarmament or even a "freeze" on nuclear testing without knowing what the opponent was going to do? This kind of recommendation would be suicidal, and the Judeo-Christian tradition frowns on suicide. NATO generals, whatever their religious principles might tell them, should frown on it too.

If the generals demand a religious perspective on nuclear weapons, then they would be well advised to consult the pope's views. Pope John Paul II has argued that "in current conditions 'deterrence' based on balance, certainly not as an end in itself but as a step on the way toward a progressive disarmament, may still be judged morally acceptable."[25] The generals—and the bishops—ignore the sound reasoning behind deterrence.

In a similar vein, the generals support NATO leader William Rogers, who chastises President Reagan for seeking "nuclear superiority." The president has made no bones about his nuclear policy: "Our military strength is a prerequisite to peace, but we hope this strength will never be used."[26] Amen. The generals offer us a kind of statement now familiar and glorified in nuclear policy circles. In effect it says that by being stronger militarily, you will actually be worse off. Superiority, whether you realize it or not, is actually inferiority. Yes, and war is peace, love is hate, and $2 + 2 = 5$. It is spellbinding to investigate the "informed" opinions on nuclear weaponry and to find how many of them rest on a foundation of antilogic.

Nearly as common are views that place all the blame on Americans. One would think the deployment of Pershing and cruise missiles in Europe would have caused general ease on that continent. Instead, the United States is accused of "breaking off negotiations" with the Soviet Union. Fancy that! The Soviets have missiles targeted on every major European city, and the Americans are "disruptive" for trying to establish a balance of power. The generals follow this with the mysterious statement, "The United States' potential deployed in Europe is no longer a deterrent."[27] Does this imply that it once was a deterrent but that cruise missiles no longer inspire fear—that although the Soviets were once afraid of incineration, they have managed to get over it? Have the Soviets attacked Western Europe with its "impotent" NATO deployment? The conclusion is pure fantasy. Consider that the Soviets are unafraid of missiles that could strike deep into their territory in about six minutes. Annihilation, once a deterrent to aggression, no longer deters. Perhaps the missiles don't deter because they are U.S. missiles. God deliver us from the absurd notion that the United States is always on the wrong side in foreign policy matters.

Finally, the generals stated, "It is imperative to give up a nuclear defense in Central Europe if we want to survive."[28] This is supported, I gather, by an earlier statement: "Security based on strength is a threat to international security."[29] Paradoxically, our Pershings and cruises increase our chances of dying. Strength is not strength. Those who support this "scare argument" would waste no time in scrapping the U.S. nuclear arsenal in NATO while the Soviets maintain theirs.

European nightmares about U.S. nuclear weapons are not new. They have always been ambivalent about nuclear weaponry. However, it is new—and a cause for wonder—that NATO statesmen adopt views about military policy very similar to those of the Soviets. Melvyn Krauss pointed out:

The message the Europeans appear to be sending the Kremlin is this: "We will close our eyes to the horror you do in Afghanistan and Poland. We will enrich you by increased trade and subsidies. We will conspire with you to obstruct the Americans in Central America and frustrate their efforts to build a strategic defense. We will do all this and all we will ask in return is for you not to invade us."[30]

Krauss suggested that NATO is accommodating the Soviet Union by allowing Soviet views to seep into NATO policy. The situation suggests fear, and the symptoms of that fear imply that Stockholm Syndrome has gained a strong foothold in Western Europe.

George Kennan once said, "You don't need to occupy a country to dominate its life."[31] The threat of an invasion, by itself, has been sufficient to turn Western Europe into a hostage, into a continent that adopts policies that give the Soviet Union much of what it wants without having to flex its trigger finger.

These threatening weapons have every bit as much potential to create fear as the finger on the trigger of the hijacker's machine gun. Their ability to paralyze the will and scramble reason can be measured by citing the conclusions of some of the most renowned English-speaking experts in the world.

Kennan is a case in point. Not long after World War II Kennan concluded that the United States should protect those areas that "we cannot permit to fall into enemy hands." That was the early Kennan. That was the same Kennan who argued against sharing nuclear secrets with the Soviets. In a now famous dispatch sent to the secretary of state from Moscow one month after Hiroshima, Kennan wrote:

There is nothing—I repeat nothing—in the history of the Soviet regime which could justify us in assuming that the men who are now in power in Russia, or even those who have chances of assuming power in the foreseeable future, would hesitate for a moment to apply this power against us if by doing so they thought they might materially improve their own power position in the world. . . . To assume that the Soviets would be restrained by scruples of gratitude or humanitarianism would be to fly in the face of overwhelming contrary evidence on a matter vital to the security of our country.[32]

Not more than a year later, Kennan urged the United States to promote the development of both biological and atomic weapons.

For Kennan, this view has gone the way of the dinosaur. He now derides the common belief that if U.S. weaponry were removed from Europe, the Soviets would subject NATO countries to various forms of nuclear blackmail. Kennan provides no argument to back his view that this kind of Soviet expansionism is a "myth." The earlier Kennan wouldn't have dared to label the possibility a myth. Are there any signs, after thirty consecutive years of arms buildups and activities beyond their borders, that the Soviets have mellowed, thereby making the conquest of NATO countries a myth? Has Kennan asked NATO or U.S. leaders if they think the possibility of Soviet expansion into Western Europe is a myth? In Kennan's mind the Soviets must have changed from being a "menace" in the early postwar years to being a nonthreatening regime that only happens to stockpile weapons in warehouses, to give out false statistics about them, and to aim the weapons at European nations. Hence, he now advises us that "Reduction of nuclear arsenals, not their multiplication, leads to security."[33] He also maintains, "Nuclear weapons are not 'true weapons' and . . . they are 'the most useless weapons ever invented.' "[34] All of this may be true regarding actual use, but are we to dismantle weapons while an enemy nation still retains them?

Douglas Lackey, a philosopher in the City University of New York, said yes. On the whole, Lackey argued, more lives would be preserved throughout the world if we adopted a policy of unilateral disarmament. But how is this recommendation different from "better red than dead"?[35] If either we or Europe disarm, the likelihood that the Soviets might strike against both is increased. What ability would we have to retaliate? If the Soviets didn't launch an all-out strike, they could still practice nuclear blackmail or even destroy any military facilities that would enable a besieged nation to recover its nuclear capability. No, unilateral disarmament is a great danger.

In *The Nuclear Crisis Reader* former navy admiral Eugene Carroll contributed his own specious reasoning to the debate. He gave us five principles that "offer promise for the future." Most notable among these principles are numbers 1 and 5: (1) "Nuclear weapons serve no useful purpose" (which he only supports by calling on the authority of Lord Mountbatten)[36]; (5) "People are deterred from war by many factors, of which military power is only one."[37] These principles conflict. If nuclear weaponry deters, then the weapons do serve a military purpose, even if the purpose is not of the traditional kind. Their utility lies in their not being used.

Nor does it make sense to conclude, "War will come, or will be averted, entirely without respect to any consideration of nuclear 'superiority.'"[38] This is also an antideterrence argument, which Carroll floated without evidence. He said, "The normal, traditional issues and interests which govern international relations and political decisions" will be "dominant." But these traditional factors may very well be overridden by the fear of nuclear retaliation. After all, deterrence means having such a balance of forces that any gains that one side contemplates are far outweighted by the losses they would incur.

Again, we are told that there is "no sensible military use" for any kind of nuclear weapon. But several pages later, Carroll wrote, "The usefulness of a strategic capability is that of deterrence." Which is it?

Besides these contradictions, we are also subject to several limping analogies. Professor Michael McGwire reminds us of the concerned body politic who "counter" defense "buildup" policy: "It's like the man who is obsessed with the danger of a meteor strike, and steadily increases the thickness of his roof until the house collapses with his family inside."[39] What this means I don't know. It could mean that military defense is as fruitless as making a fort out of your house. But I will give McGwire and the enlightened "body politic" the benefit of the doubt and say that it must mean something deeper. Only they could tell us. Another view compares the gathering of nuclear weapons to drug addiction. Evidently, the only logical requirement in the nuclear debate is that you have something more different and stranger to say than the last person who spoke.

To the psychologist Karl Meminger's assessment that both the Soviets and the Americans are "piling up rocks like little children," I agree. But until both sides agree on a mutual minimum deterrent, the United States and NATO should continue to maintain their present rock pile. Rather than reduce arsenals in the United States and Europe for the sake of reducing, we should take Richard Pipes's advice to heart: "All considerations of nuclear weapons should be reduced to the nature and extent of the Soviet threat: any statement on the subject of weapons and strategy that fails to address itself to this central subject should be dismissed as irrelevant."[40] In that case many of the aforementioned analyses of our nuclear policies in NATO should be consigned to the flames where they will do the most good.

European minds are often deeply confused about the role of nuclear weapons. The Social Democratic party of West Germany has rejected nuclear weaponry as part of its official platform. Protestors throughout Europe argue that the United States is "using" Europe for its own private war against the Soviets. According to one German "expert," Konrad Keller, "Many Germans reason that the Pershings make it possible to have a nuclear war between the Soviet Union and Western Europe without any United States involvement."[41] Has Mr. Keller contemplated what the absence of Pershings would allow the Soviets to do? These long-range missiles stay a Soviet advance into Western Europe. They provide a deterrent.

Another statement that ignores the "deterrent factor" of the U.S. guarantee is one made by Oxford University's Michael Howard. He reasoned, "So far from Americans being in Europe to help the Europeans to defend themselves, they are seen in some quarters as being here to prosecute 'their' war—a war in which the Europeans have no interest and for which they are the first to suffer."[42]

Howard's insight makes it sound like the United States wants war. It is this kind of rabble-rousing conclusion that fuels the protest movement, not to mention nuclear fright and general misunderstanding. The U.S. presence in Europe surely does not signify a desire for war. Instead, these armaments are placed to stop a war, a war that would threaten U.S. interests globally.

German Countess Marion Donhoff does Howard one better. "Europe," she said, "is frightened more by the United States than by the Russians." A deeply felt brand of anti-Americanism is evidenced in West Germany. John Vinocur wrote in the *International Herald Tribune*:

Intellectuals such as Gunter Grass, in the heat of the debate on new NATO missiles, said they felt shame for America, which they pictured as an oafish, discredited bully. . . . [This] view trickled through the layers of the mass media. A typical book of pop politics, written by Peter Merseberger, presented the United States as a reeling, incalculable force from which the Germans must keep their distance. It is not just that "America has a permanent taste for violence," that it has a "lower horizon of political expectations" than Europe; that it admires Walt Whitman, "the bard of American imperialism"; that it is a "disturbed, rudderless" place; but that—by the television reporter's definition—it is deeply, organically flawed and dangerous.[43]

West German resentment of the United States goes further than any controversy over Pershing and cruise missiles. The presence of 340,000 U.S. troops in West Germany reminds the Europeans that they lean on the United States for their freedom, on a nation that defeated them in a war only forty years before.

Other voices in Europe evidence a deepening anticommunist sentiment. In France Andre Glucksman, a former leading figure in the Communist party, has turned against the increasingly disreputable Communist party with a vengeance. Glucksman is at odds with "peace protestors," who in their fragmented vision have made nuclear war into the only great evil of our time. Glucksman likes to say there are two evils: Nuclear catastrophe is one; the Gulag, the other. Yes, a nuclear war would destroy life. But Glucksman responds to those who dwell on this fact and who, therefore, fear bombs more than camps, by asking, "What does it mean for life to survive? Doesn't human life require some modicum of political liberty to be worth talking about? Human beings have a soul, not just a body, and the soul too, must have a life." Instead of accepting the Gulag out of fear of the bomb, Glucksman accepts the bomb out of fear of the Gulag.

Despite the sound, invincible wisdom of Glucksman's ideas, many "survival-is-enough-types" think that the German acquisition of nuclear weapons would be so provocative to the Soviet Union that it could cause the Kremlin to launch an attack against West Germany. Again, we have an argument equal to "better Red than dead." This is nuclear nonsense. More than that, it is unadulterated idiocy. The Soviets do not know how the United States would react to an attack on West Germany. Nor do they wish to find out.

Fear of the Soviet Union also overwhelms former German Chancellor Helmut Schmidt. In his book, *A Grand Strategy for the West*, Schmidt gave us his best geopolitical thinking:

West Germany is a small country about the size of an average American state, say Oregon or Colorado. . . . Think of people in Oregon having seven different armies and 5,000 foreign nuclear weapons deployed on their soil, and the Russians that close. It takes the Soviet fighter bombers just five minutes to appear in the sky above Hamburg.[44]

This is poignant, but that is all. The same logic would make Americans fear the proximity of Soviet ballistic missiles, which would take only thirty minutes to reach the United States. But proximity is not the issue. Nuclear weapons make every target a close one. It is a poor argument not to assemble a deterrent force just because the other side is so near.

The very conclusions of these statesmen and experts reveal that fright and unconscious fears of the darkest kind are playing with our judgments about how to take care of our security and NATO's. What else could explain why the most logical considerations are ignored while the most frightened attitudes are recommended? Westerners who are most knowledgeable are guilty of what Andre Sakharov called, "playing by the Soviet rules of the game."[45] Not only are the aforementioned generals, protestors, intellectuals, and statesmen prey to this threat, but so are the strongest leaders of NATO countries. In the next chapter we will examine Soviet policy in Europe and its effect on the decisions, opinions, and behavior of West Europeans.

In *NATO in Transition*, Mr. Stanley suggested what might happen if there were ever a "de-coupling" of U.S. power from Europe: "For if they set in motion a separatist trend, or if political factors . . . dominate, Europe may in fact become the hostage which the Soviets already claim it has."[46]

Stanley did not use the term "hostage" as completely as I do. He suggested nothing more than a military hostage. I observe that Europe is already psychologically hostage to the Soviet Union.

How have the Soviets accomplished this? That is the question I will address in the following chapters.

# 5

# *Soviet Policy*

The policy of Peaceful Coexistence is . . . a form of intense economic, political, and ideological struggle between the proletariat and the aggressive forces of imperialism in the world arena.[1]

-Nikita Khrushchev

Khrushchev, during his long reign at the helm of the Soviet political ship, repeatedly warned the Communist movement not to expect victory in their goal of world conquest through the devices of a major war. He warned them against such an expectation not because such a war would be costly and dangerous, but because, in his words, "Victory could be achieved without it."

The Soviet Union long ago created and has long since supported a vast network of proxies throughout the world that carry out her bidding. Through them, the Soviet Union has been able to mount and support continuously communist insurrections, worldwide student protests, terrorist activities, and chaos. A fundamental part of their long-term strategy, while it precludes a major war, is to continue to fight and support "just" wars: "There will be liberation wars as long as imperialism exists, as long as colonialism exists. Wars of this kind are revolutionary wars. Such wars are not only justified but inevitable."[2]

Bejamin Netanyahu, permanent representative of Israel to the United Nations, writing on terrorism, explained:

The Soviet-PLO connection hardly needs documentation, as PLO leaders have publicly acknowledged that thousands of Fedayeen have been trained in Russia. The Soviet Union has given the PLO operatives special movement throughout East Europe.

But the most striking testimony of involvement in international terrorism comes from the Czechoslovakian defector, General Jan Sejna. Sejna said that he was personally involved in a training program in Czechoslovakia under the direct control of Soviet military intelligence (the GRV). Sejna provided details of the training and names of the Italians who had been through the program. Included among them were well-known figures in the Red Brigade such as Feltrinelli and Franchesini and others who were unknown at the time but who subsequently turned out to be important terrorists.[3]

This is at the crux of what the Soviets mean by "a policy of peaceful coexistence." The message to the adherents of communism continues though. The Communist party platform has warned the faithful as to what peaceful coexistence certainly does not mean: specifically, it does not imply renunciation of the class struggle.

No end to class struggle. No end to revolutionary wars. No end to the continued support of all manners and means that will foster a constant state of chaos. Peaceful coexistence? Perhaps not, but such a course of action is guaranteed to continue to put pressure on the allies and to maintain a high level of stress in the world.

Nations at times define peace to suit themselves. The Nomenklatura, the Soviet leadership, goes by a definition of peace that is the most minimal definition possible. Peace means nothing more than a condition in which nations do not shoot at one another. Any other kind of hostility is thought to be quite consistent with peace—ideological warfare, for example, which involves hatred; or class war, which opposes one social group against another; or wars of national liberation. In short, the concept of peace employed by the Nomenklatura matches the hostage taker's concept of peace: Peace allows for all manner of hostilities except shooting. Everything besides physical harm fits this definition of peace.

Peace under détente left people with a similar impression. Henry Kissinger, in his book *Nuclear Weapons and Foreign Policy*,[4] was severely critical of the concept of peaceful coexistence. Kissinger felt that the Soviets took peaceful coexistence to mean nothing more than "the most effective offensive tactic" and "the best means to subvert the existing structure by means other than all-out-war." The Leninist doctrine the Soviets followed was clear: So long as the balance of power was not in their favor, they should keep "provocation" below the level that might produce a final showdown.

Eight years later, in 1965, Kissinger had more criticism of "detente peace." It was "futile" to engage in "personal diplomacy" with the Soviets, "even at the highest level," for whenever Soviet leaders have had to make a choice between Western good will and a territorial or political gain, "they have unhesitatingly chosen the latter." He noted five periods of Soviet "relaxation" since 1917, all of which ended for the same reason—"when an opportunity for expanding communism presented itself."[5]

After 1972, when Brezhnev and Nixon signed the "Basic Principles of Agreement" initiating détente, Kissinger could only say that détente had limited the risks of nuclear conflict. Senator J. William Fulbright agreed: "Detente, in its essence, is an agreement not to let superpower differences explode into nuclear war."[6]

If this was peace under détente, then perhaps détente was a euphemism for cold war. In both eras the conflict between the superpowers fell short of actual war.

Both détente and cold war are accordion terms; they can be pulled this way and that until they mean just about anything except nuclear war. In this vein, a French journalist paraphrased Clausewitz's famous statement, "War is the pursuit of diplomacy by other means," into "detente is the Cold War pursued by other means—and sometimes the same." Theodore Draper, a noted historian and political analyst, reminds us of Lenin's favorite formulation of the most important political question: "Kto kogo?"—literally, "Who does what to whom?" Draper concluded his estimation of the subject in saying, "This is not a bad way to think about detente."[7] We will further analyze the importance of détente in Chapter 7. For now we will look at what the Soviet strategic goals are in Europe.

The Soviet goal is not subtle. It does not require a great mind to uncover their designs of world conquest. Yet, the threat that they will do anything to achieve that end seems to lie outside Europe's reality framework. Professor Michael McGwire thought that the Soviet Union has "no urge to seize Western Europe," and he used this conclusion to attack NATO's doctrine of nuclear deterrence.[8] Since historical facts show that the Soviet Union has no strong urge to territorial expansion, McGwire said they can have no temptation to seize Western Europe. Temptation, in McQwire's mind, is the sum of both the "opportunity" for successful action and the "urge" to take such action. In short, there is no need to match the Soviet capability of waging war, since the Soviets lack the urge to move against Europe.

One cannot imagine what led McGwire to say that the temptation to take Europe has declined since the 1950s. What kinds of facts McGwire requires are not clear. As Pipes argued, there is certainly an economic motivation for the Soviets to conquer Western Europe. Since Western European nations have a combined gross national product greater than the United States, a conquest of Europe would allow the Soviets to solve their economic problems in one fell swoop. McGwire's thinking flies into the teeth of the evidence: Soviet leaders have admitted a desire to seek a rapprochement with Western Europe that excludes the United States. Judging by the views of others, like George Kennan and many Europeans, McGwire is not alone in his attributing nonexpansionism to the Soviets.

Khrushchev knew early on that Europe would always doubt the truth of the Soviet Union's goal and will to achieve it. He knew that they would run to the "peacemaker." From this knowledge emanated Khrushchev's confidence that the Soviets would achieve their goal without having to fight in a major war.[9]

Khrushchev promised the communists victory. How could he promise that and at the same time tell them that they would not have to fight a major war to achieve it? Because he knew that it would not be necessary.

That is the underlying knowledge of the Soviet strategists. The Soviets know their victory will come more from their arms buildup than from the use of these weapons. Arsenals breed fear. The Soviets will continue to support wars and revolutions that they believe are just, not because they really care about the proletariat but because they know that such wars breed chaos, which in turn heightens the stress level in the world.

The historical record leaves no doubt about warlike threats the Soviets have used against the Europeans. Scandinavian members of NATO were threatened that they would "burn in the fire of a nuclear war fought in the name of Atlantic solidarity."[10] The 1983 German election of Helmut Kohl, the Soviets said, could result in West Germany's "ascending a nuclear gallows."[11] Similarly, a deployment of U.S. ground-launched cruise missiles would convert all of Italy into a "Pompei."[12] Despite this sort of unmistakable nuclear blackmail, the foreign ministers of Italy, Spain, the Federal Republic of Germany, and the president of France himself all visited Moscow during the first two months of Chernenko's rule as Soviet leader. In spite of this evidence, we have advisers and "experts" arguing that there is no Soviet motivation to conquer Europe and sever the alliance, that in fact such a motivation is "insane" (Kennan).[13] It appears that no amount of evidence can convince these people. They deny Soviet intentions even though the Soviets continually play the anti-American side of the street in Europe and are forever trying to negotiate deals with NATO leaders with the United States on the sidelines.

Andrei Sakharov warned of the peril of accepting the Soviet "rules of the game." But this wise advice fell on deaf ears, perhaps because its implications are unclear. As Pipes saw it, "Manipulation of the international rules of conflict to its exclusive benefit, against a general climate of nuclear terror, is one of the most effective and least noted tools of Soviet foreign policy."[14] What effect does this have on the behavior of those in the Soviet sphere of influence? Pipes argued that a strong connection exists between a state of "terror driven fear" in a nation and a tendency for that nation to be politically exploited.

One of the few persons who analyzed this connection is the Swiss writer Urs Schwarz. Schwarz drew an illuminating distinction between fear, which he defined as a normal and healthy response to an identifiable threat that produces a defensive reaction, and anxiety, which is a more or less constant condition of fear, focused on no particular threat, and liable to feed on itself and paralyze the will. About the fear generated by nuclear weapons he said:

> That the danger in the technical sense is real and that the accumulated forces of destruction are monstrous requires neither emphasis nor proof. One knows [the dangers] and has every reason to be deeply concerned. But the attitude of the majority of people toward those facts is not one of fear or of concern but of pronounced anxiety. . . . It is precisely in this connection that the distinction between fear and anxiety assumes great significance. While fear is an entirely desirable reaction to the threat of nuclear weapons, because it makes possible the reaction of deterrence and thereby prevents war, anxiety can produce the contrary effect.[15]

Constant anxiety can lead to lack of resolve, weakness, and a predisposition to alleviate that anxiety by accommodating one's opponent. This is the dynamic operating in Western Europe, which can only give encouragement to the Soviets.

The rationale behind the Soviet belief in victory without fighting a major war seems to be beyond the vision of Western strategists. While the West debates whether to arm itself in response to the rapid arms buildup of the Soviets, the Soviets come in the back door and undermine the West by use of its psychological arsenal.

Europe is hostage, and the Soviets haven't had to fire a single bullet at them in order to accomplish it. The evidence for this is nearly as vast as the continent of Europe. Europeans act with greater and greater accommodation toward the Soviets. They behave and hold opinions that show they are under the gun. They possess what Schwarz called a healthy fear of the Soviet arsenal, but they also possess the anxiety that leads them to identify with the Soviets.

This identification with the aggressor is the first phase of Stockholm Syndrome. The second phase brings about the rejection of outside interference, the repudiation of a third-person authority like the police. In this case the police are the United States. Paradoxically, more and more Europeans believe that the United States forms the real threat to their security and is the true cause of international tension. Europe in the 1980s languishes in the second phase of Stockholm Syndrome, attributing stress-causing aggression more to the United States than to the Soviets. Recall Countess Marion Donhoff's statement: "Europe is frightened more by the United States than the Russians."[16]

Moreover, in a Rand Corporation study Peter Schmidt surmised that "the most critical development in West Germany is an increasing belief that the U.S.S.R. is looking for reconciliation with the West and a decreasing belief that the United States is acting much more responsibly than the U.S.S.R."[17] The fact that so many West Germans see so little difference between the United States and the Soviet Union is indeed disquieting. Further, Pipes pointed out that 40 percent of West Germans unconditionally oppose the stationing of nuclear weapons on their soil, regardless of how many the Soviets have.[18]

The bond between Soviet and European leaders is already forming. NATO leaders are careful not to give offense to the Soviets in word or deed. Their opinions are carefully muted so as not to appear in conflict with Soviet views. Even at times when a harsh rebuke of Soviet recklessness seems in order, European leaders back down. After several instances of Soviet adventurism, U.S. policy called for grain, technology, and general trade sanctions against the Soviets. But the NATO response was fragmented. On some occasions NATO countries made up for the U.S. trade embargoes by increasing their own exports to the East.

The placement of nuclear weapons is also a divisive issue. The unpopularity of U.S. weapons on NATO soil is comparable to the unpopularity of the police in a hostage situation. With the increased attraction of leftist parties—like the Greens in West Germany and the Labour party in Great Britain—some analysts believe that U.S. weaponry will be removed from European soil before long, leaving the allies with only a weak conventional force to battle the much stronger communist bloc conventional forces. Prudent reflection dictates that the nuclear weapons should remain in Western Europe, if only to prevent a Soviet move to occupy Europe or deter a Soviet nuclear strike. But rationality is proving to be no match for the heated anxiety that a large percentage of the European electorate and leaders are feeling.

The U.S. arsenal is in place to counteract the Soviet missiles aimed at every major West European city. Incredibly, the prevalent European belief is that U.S. forces do the opposite of what they are supposed to do: U.S. missiles endanger NATO countries and increase the chances of a nuclear exchange! Europeans are in the grip of the unconscious behavior familiar to Stockholm Syndrome; Europe acts like an unwitting hostage of the Soviet Union.

Specific events as well as general tendencies solidify this view of hostage Europe. All who oppose this analysis bear the burden of explaining the following:

- Why are Europeans so driven to negotiate treaties—especially arms control treaties—with the Soviets, even when these treaties seem opposed to NATO's interests and even when substantial negotiating progress gives way to political atmospherics?

- Why were NATO leaders disturbed by the U.S. decision to cease abiding by the unratified SALT II treaty, when the record shows consistent violations of the treaty by the Soviets?

- Why has West Germany not only rejected U.S. nuclear weaponry but also adopted a policy of nonretaliation, even in the event of a Soviet nuclear strike? Further, if this is their policy, why would they let it be known?

- Why has there been a surge of neo-Gaullism—or avowed independence from the alliance—in West Germany and France?

- How is it that European behavior follows a strict ratio: The stronger the U.S. line toward the Soviet Union, the more Europe becomes independent of the alliance?

- Why did Helmut Schmidt in 1979 declare that he would gladly accept nuclear weapons on his soil if and only if another NATO nation followed suit?

- What leads French President Francois Mitterrand to go on record for taking a stronger anti-NATO line than even Charles de Gaulle?

- How could German intellectual Gunter Grass make the analogy that the United States, by stationing nuclear bases in Europe, is behaving toward Europe like Rome did toward its provinces?[19]

- Why did French and German leaders allow steel contractors to make multibillion dollar sales of pipes and oil rigs after the Soviet invasion of Afghanistan, thereby passing up the opportunity to use economic leverage on the Soviets?

- By what logic could French leader Debre call the invasion of Afghanistan "a traffic accident on the road to detente"?[20]

• How could NATO nations, with their avowed fear of "decoupling" from the United States, on the one hand, consistently misread Soviet designs to divide the alliance, on the other?

For anyone denying the increasing spirit of compliance and tendency for identification on the part of the Western Europeans, these eleven questions are a formidable obstacle.

The questions grow in number all the time. Such events as the shoot-down of the KAL-007 airliner, the Chernobyl nuclear accident, and the kidnapping of Daniloff occur with very little rebuke from the Europeans. The retaliatory bombing of Libya didn't cause Europe to use sanctions against that country, but it did lead Europeans to criticize the United States. On the whole, the allies dislike U.S. assertiveness and would prefer that the United States adopt a mild, conciliatory, live-and-let-live attitude toward the Soviets. With each new U.S. criticism of Soviet behavior our allies drift even closer to neutrality and accommodation with them.

West Germany is a paradigm example. A good part of the German public desires a friendly association with the United States only on the condition that this relationship not irritate the Soviet Union. A recent poll showed that 53 percent of the German population consider "good relations with the United States" essential for the security of the West, which happens to be a higher proportion than in any other NATO nation (only 25 percent of the British hold this opinion)![21] Moreover, there is a solid majority among Germans in favor of collaborating and aligning with the West. But the bottom line is that this holds true only as long as the Soviets are excluded from the equation and the choice is a simple either/or: for NATO and the United States or without them. When the situation is complicated by the inclusion of the Soviet Union's interests, Germany grows reluctant to do anything anti-Soviet. Thus, some 40 percent of the Germans oppose the stationing of nuclear weapons on their soil, quite irrespective of whether the Soviets deploy and target their missiles on Germany. With this kind of neutralist attitude, even conservatives in the United States wish to reconsider the U.S. commitment to NATO.

Pipes complained of "the inequitable distribution of responsibilities within the alliance."[22] With Germany, Great Britain, and France growing increasingly neutralist, what justification is there for the United States to spend 6 percent of its GNP each year on defense—approximately 56 percent of which goes toward the defense of Europe—$135 billion a year. Meanwhile, the European countries spend at most 3 percent and Japan less than 1 percent of their GNP on military. When this kind of a commitment to Europe is coupled with European appeasement of the Soviets, the mind begins to boggle. No wonder that persons as different as Henry Kissinger, Sam Nunn, and Melvyn Krauss recommend that the United States withdraw its military commitment to NATO. Of that, I shall say more later.

At present, the dominant political situations in Britain and West Germany are significant for European–U.S. and European–Soviet relations. The opposition parties of both countries have undergone a shift to the left. If these parties have their day, Western Europe will be moving away from the United States and toward the Soviet Union. Some Germans still entertain the possibility of striking up a deal with the Soviet Union that will lead to a process of gradual unification between East and West Germany. The price for such an agreement? A withdrawal from NATO.

There is an increasing desire on the part of Europeans to be independent from NATO. In France, the foreign policy of former President Valéry Giscard d'Estaing clearly took its inspiration from the legacy left by de Gaulle, who promoted an independent French policy. However, this independence had a catch to it. Giscard d'Estaing's policy was that if France ever found itself in desperate need, it reserved the right to call on its allies for help. If the allies asked France for help, however, France could refuse because it was not "aligned." As Theodore Draper sarcastically wrote, "An alliance that does not align is a mystery of the French language."

Current French President Francois Mitterrand has gone even further in his freedom from alliance. In October 1980 Mitterrand completed his book, *La drole d'alliance*, or *The Phony Alliance*.[23] Many critical statements about the NATO partnership were made by Mitterrand:

- There is no Atlantic alliance, or more exactly . . . it no longer has any meaning.
- France "left" [quotation marks are my own, since France has not completely left] NATO, which placed her in a position of dependence on the Pentagon, without suffering any other punishment than bad temper. We have gone out of it, and we won't go back to it.
- I have a desire to cry out: enough hypocrisies, enough of the American hypocrisy which reduces its allies to the status of satellites in exchange for a hypothetical protection.
- The Soviet machine bungles, and America is no longer a reliable partner for anyone.
- I have not chosen either Russia or America. I am trying to confront this double danger.

These views of the alliance are more severe than anything de Gaulle would have said when he removed France from the alliance. And while France has continued to embrace Gaullism under Pompidou, Giscard d'Estaing, and Mitterrand, similar balancing acts were occurring in West Germany.

Willy Brandt, Social Democratic foreign minister of West Germany, described Germany's precarious situation in the early 1970s: "Our national interest does not permit us to stand between East and West. Our country needs cooperation and harmonization with the West and understanding with the East."[24] Brandt enigmatically defined this "understanding" as "partnership": "Russia is inextricably woven into the history of Europe, not only as an adversary and danger but also as a partner—historical, political, cultural and economic."[25] Gaullism, then, was certainly not peculiar to the French. Germany under Helmut Schmidt revealed more of the same.

When the Iraq–Iran war started on September 22, 1980, all the allies had a pressing national interest in keeping the oil flowing from the Persian Gulf area. Indeed, the Europeans had vested interests in the gulf far greater than those of the United States. France and Germany get one half of their oil from the gulf, while the United States gets only one eighth of its oil there. Yet when President Carter suggested a few days after the outbreak that the allied and interested powers should hold a conference to discuss the conflict, the immediate response from Chancellor Schmidt was enough to sink the proposal. Schmidt, who was once referred to as "the most powerful man in Europe West of Mr. Brezhnev," chose to interpret the West German Constitution in such a way that it prohibited him from participating in allied action in the Persian Gulf area. The proposed conference was never mentioned again. Draper pointed out, "No doubt more will be heard of the demand that the United States should consult her allies."[26]

A prominent international affairs expert, Uwe Nerlich surmised: "Unlike the 1950s and to some extent the 1960s there is today almost an absence of distinctly pro-American political parties in Western Europe. . . . A positive stand on preferential cooperation with the United States is not currently seen to pay political dividends."[27] Nerlich concluded that close ties with the United States are the single most important foreign relations of any West European member state. How these contradictory impulses—that the United States is both important yet unpopular—can exist side by side remains a frustrating riddle to many.

My conclusion is that only fear could lead the Europeans to be so lukewarm and systematically ambivalent. The fear is of a threat from the Soviet Union. The Europeans respond to this threat with continuous and unconscious anxiety. NATO countries believe a preferred stance is one that doesn't anger the Soviets. To some observers, this is an expression of "Euro-détente." To me, it smacks of "Euro-wimpery," for whenever European leaders are justified in siding with Atlantic interests, their very first consideration is, Will this position give offense to the Soviets? European leaders have anticipated and internalized the Soviet Union's reactions.

Nowhere does this reflex hold more true than in military issues—in decisions involving invasions, war, and nuclear weaponry. In the 1973 October War in the Middle East, Henry Kissinger's strategy for maintaining a balance of power depended on a massive airlift of supplies to the Israeli forces, which had sustained heavy losses from the initial Egyptian surprise attack. One ally after another refused to allow its territory to be used for refueling stops for the U.S. airlift. In Washington recriminations followed Willy Brandt's refusal to allow Israeli freighters to pick up U.S. arms at Bremerhaven (which would have violated German neutrality) or to permit U.S. planes to overfly German territory on the way to the Middle East, which resulted in U.S. pilots flying a 2,000-mile detour. Kissinger completed his testimony before the House Foreign Affairs Committee with an unofficial aside: "I don't care what happens to NATO; I'm so disgusted."[28]

To Kissinger, European criticisms of U.S. policy followed a "damned if you do, damned if you don't" kind of logic. The United States could not hide from European disapproval. If the administration in Washington was not being blamed for stirring things up, then it was being accused of "dividing the world" with détente. Friendly relations between the United States and the Soviet Union struck the Europeans as being even more dangerous than the hard line for which the Reagan administration is now criticized.

In the détente era, the more that Nixon and Brezhnev talked peace, the more Europe felt left out in the cold. The Europeans feared "decoupling"—being left alone by the United States to face the East. But when requests were made for a unified response to exert pressure on the Soviet Union, the Europeans remained noncommittal.

The invasion of Afghanistan was a case in point. Soon after Afghanistan was invaded, Giscard and Schmidt went to Moscow to talk privately with Brezhnev! As I said before, French statesmen

Debre chimed in with his estimation that the death of 130,000 people in the invasion was but "a traffic accident on the road to detente." Looking back at this kind of response, writer Arch Puddington was moved say, "Those who are predisposed to a favorable analysis of the Soviets seem to be very capable of ignoring, forgetting about or explaining away acts of Soviet barbarism."[29]

And Zbigniew Brzezinski noted that when the Solidarity movement was crushed in Poland several years later, such leading West German spokesmen as former Chancellor Helmut Schmidt and editor Theo Summer publicly endorsed the action, in marked contrast to the condemnation with which it was received by other West European socialists.

In a speech on April 10, 1980, President Carter threw up his hands in frustration, voiced his disappointment, and crystallized all that seemed wrong with the alliance:

- Nations ask us for leadership. But at the same time they demand their own independence of action.
- They ask us for aid. But they reject any interference.
- They ask us for understanding, but they often decline to understand us in return.
- Some ask for protection, but are wary of the obligation of alliance.
- Others ask for firmness and certainty. But at the same time, they demand the flexibility required by the pace of change and the subtlety of events.[30]

Professor Hans Morgenthau concluded that if one side "receives the lion's share of the benefits but the other the bulk of the burdens, then such an alliance is indistinguishable from a treaty of guarantee."[31] This was certainly the nature of the original alliance: European members were allies only in their own self-defense. But our focus is slightly different. The attitudes and behavior of the allies are void of consistency or rationality. Europeans had joined the alliance because they resembled a sick patient in need of a doctor. Now the patient turns the doctor down, even though their behavior reveals that the illness still exists. The illness must be brought to their attention.

During Carter's tenure opinion polls in Europe reflected high approval for his human rights stand against the Soviet Union—79 percent in West Germany and 68 percent in France supported him. European leaders held a different opinion. When Leonid Brezhnev denounced President Carter for receiving Soviet dissidents in the White House and carrying on "psychological warfare" against his regime, the president expressed surprise that his moral concerns should damage U.S.–Soviet relations. Instead of backing Carter in this incident, Helmudt Schmidt felt confirmed in his view that the president was hopefully naïve. He denounced Carter for acting "like a faith healer," not a leader. In France, Giscard said that Carter's action "compromised the spirit of detente."[32] In other words, in the minds of these leaders even ethical considerations took a back seat to pleasing the Soviets. European heads of state agreed that it was not human rights that they were against; they feared that their own domestic problems might worsen as a result of aggravating the Soviets. To Europe, this was practicing détente and exercising caution. To the United States, it was a lack of intestinal fortitude. To me, it's a sign of Stockholm Syndrome.

It sometimes seems to Americans that West Europe's behavior forms a neat comparison with Finland's. If the Finns under Soviet influence do not behave responsibly, they will threaten the survival of their own nation. Acting responsibly translates into refraining from doing anything the Soviets may not like, and this involves not only self-censorship, but also the need to anticipate Soviet wishes. The Finns are very much under Soviet influence. European leaders have not yet been Finlandized, but like the Finns, they anticipate and carry out Soviet wishes.

The subject of nuclear arms is where European appeasement of Soviet demands seems the greatest. To listen to European views about arms control, one would think that getting to the table, shaking hands, smiling, and engaging in political atmospherics is important, quite independent of whether any substantive agreements are reached. Their ideal seems to place the negotiating of treaties above all else. In the United States, too, the spirit of Christmas sweeps the air whenever superpower leaders reach the bargaining table. This is true even though the Soviets consistently have not abided by the limits of agreements. Evidence from SALT I, SALT II, and START talks show that negotiations are not sincerely approached. In the words of the French General Pierre Gallois, "The Soviets do what they want and negotiate about what you're going to do."[33]

Many opinion makers and statesmen in Europe believe that agreeing on arms reduction treaties is so important that considerations of fair dealing can be ignored. Helmudt Schmidt wrote that "the West's summit meetings have deteriorated into television events." Nonetheless, Schmidt is one among many in Europe who pushes for arms negotiations. If anyone should bring attention to the record of Soviet noncompliance with treaties, that person is roundly criticized for instigating ill will or endangering détente. On the subject of arms control fanaticism, Pipes said, "Some persons go to such lengths that instead of reprimanding the U.S.S.R. for violating arms control agreements, they accuse the United States for even bringing attention to the violation."[34]

This tendency also reared its head in the controversy concerning President Reagan's decision to scrap SALT II. Here was a treaty that President Carter chose not to ratify after the invasion of Afghanistan. Despite the buildup of Soviet missiles exceeding the treaty's demands and the refusal to allow on-site inspection of their weaponry, European opinion came down hard on Washington. In European eyes, the Reagan administration was torpedoing the last "life boat" of security for the superpowers. Many overreactions seemed to follow.

A West German liberal newspaper made the hyperbolic proclamation, "The destruction of SALT II [leads us] in the most dangerous direction since World War II."[35] Another paper in France cried, "France was not asked to give its opinion," as if U.S. nuclear policy should be subordinate to a nation that deserted the military portion of NATO nearly thirty years ago. A Swiss newspaper unabashedly joined in, saying it "deplores Washington's lack of enthusiasm for East–West detente"[36] despite the fact that détente has been buried since 1979. When one would expect European reproach to be directed at the Soviet Union, we find the United States being villified once again. Why? Because it had the audacity to bring up a record of Soviet arms control abuses. Moreover, Europeans did not try to fathom Reagan's motivations. By playing the SALT card, Reagan was forcing the hand of the Soviets to see if they were interested in more serious arms negotiations.

Parties now calling for the removal of U.S. nuclear weapons in Europe are engaging in the most irresponsible decision making imaginable. A recent report in the *Economist* shows that the conventional arms on the central front might not withstand a communist bloc attack.[37] The best chance in a conventional exchange would be a war that lasted for more than four weeks. Even then, the superior numbers of conventional forces in the Warsaw Pact are very threatening. So if nuclear weaponry is removed from European soil, a safeguard against attack is removed with them.

Britain being without nuclear weaponry will make Europe more of a hostage to Soviet will. The Soviets will have all the leverage they desire in Western Europe. In addition, the United States' deterrent to Soviet aggression in Europe may no longer be credible. So the "zone-sum solution" in Western Europe will in effect translate into the "no first-use policy" that the Soviets desire and Americans loath. Instead of a steel fortress, Europe will have a paper maché defense, subject to all sorts of Soviet influences and threats. The best logical outcome would be a Europe neutralized; the worst, a Europe Finlandized.

It is simply staggering to see how many people miss this simple point. To those favoring a nuclear-free Europe, it is the weapons themselves and not the will behind them that pose the threat to peace. This is surely inaccurate. History establishes the conclusion that weakness doesn't pay. Those pushing arms control at all costs overlook the history of successful deterrence. True, we shouldn't make too much of the forty years that weapons have prevented an attack on Europe. But we shouldn't make too little of it either, at least not until a better way is arrived at. Strength repels attack. Yet a popular European periodical reports that 53 percent of Great Britain want an end to U.S. military bases in West Germany.[38] What will deter a Soviet advance if U.S. weapons are removed from British soil? Negotiations and new treaties? Has the logic of deterrence failed the British so far? How could a large percentage of the electorate want to dismantle their only shield and means of retaliation?

Deterrence works. The Soviets will only fight a war they think they can win. Winning a nuclear exchange is out of the question; the gains would be far outweighed by the losses. But a victory in conventional war is very possible due to the size and readiness of forces in the East. So a NATO nuclear deterrent now serves to dissuade even a Soviet conventional attack.

There are also differing perceptions regarding the importance of arms control. To well-meaning citizens, arms control is seen as a shortcut to peace and security. It is assumed that a reduction in forces leads to a growth in peace. However, if a lesson can be learned from the détente era, it is that the Soviets use arms control as a means to gaining strategic superiority. Moreover, no one has made a convincing case that simply reducing numbers of weapons increases security. Arms reduction should not be viewed as a vital improvement in strategic stability, although it may have a positive effect on the psychology and politics of the negotiating nations. Therefore, it is best to leave European weapons right where they are until strong evidence shows a readiness for Europeans and Warsaw alliances to reduce arms to a level of minimum assured deterrence.

European thinking about arms has been consistently inconsistent. Chancellor Schmidt worried about Soviet superiority in the central sector of Europe, since the Soviets had about 750 medium-range ballistic missiles that had no NATO counterpart. Schmidt also worried that the United States and the Soviets were immune to nuclear threat because of the balance of intercontinental missiles and that this would leave Europe as the focus for a nuclear exchange. He welcomed U.S. missiles.

Before Schmidt ever voiced his views, the United States was developing a program for European missiles to offset the backfire bombers and SS-20s of the Soviets. Recommendations were significant—572 nuclear missiles for Europe: 108 Pershing II missiles and 96 cruise missiles in the Federal Republic of Germany; 160 cruise missiles in the United Kingdom; 112 cruise missiles in Italy; and 48 cruise missiles each in the Netherlands and Belgium. The Carter administration planned to employ these weapons with a "two-track" policy: The weapons would be developed and deployed, and negotiations for their abandonment would follow.

Before the deployment, there was disagreement among European leaders, the same leaders who wanted them in the first place. Schmidt made it clear that Germany would not place the missiles unless at least one other country took them, too. Germany, he felt, could not afford to be singled out as anti-Soviet, or at least more anti-Soviet than its neighbors.

Brzezinski expressed his annoyance at Schmidt in his diary. The chancellor was indulging in "melancholy whining" about the U.S. two-track policy.[39] Behind this whining, however, were the threats from the Soviet defense minister to take "appropriate retaliatory actions" if the West went ahead with its deployment plan. Meanwhile, a new SS-20 was put into position in western and central Soviet Union every few days.

The leader of one of the major powers in Western Europe refused weapons on his soil, weighing Soviet attitudes, even while the Soviets aimed their mighty arsenal at Western Europe. Europeans are so afraid of Soviet tanks and missiles that they are hesitant to conduct Euro-détente on anything but Soviet terms—Soviet terms of "peaceful coexistence." At times it seems that the Soviets hold a seat on the NATO council.

European fear leads to other odd conclusions concerning armaments. Arms control worship in Europe leads many to believe that the United States should give the Soviet Union a blanket guarantee to adopt a no-first-use position with nuclear weapons. But this might have the unsavory consequence that the Soviet Union would seek to win a conventional war in Europe with the fear of nuclear escalation. How can we trust that a no-first-use pledge wouldn't be broken? The nuclear freeze strategy has also been trotted out by disarmament groups in Europe and by every U.S. Democrat hoping to win nomination in 1984. No-first-use and the freeze continue to be talked about by disarmament proponents. But as Brzezinski tells us, "Even the most prominent adherents (to this position) could not indicate precisely what was to be 'frozen' and how. What would be the consequences of such a freeze and a one-sided evasion of it?: In short, the issue was posed as a slogan, not a serious strategic position."[40] Indeed, once you agree to the strategy of deterrence, you cannot consistently agree to a freeze. Old weapons must be updated; new ones must be tested.

Critics of the strategic defense initiative only encourage a buildup of Soviet weapons. A *New York Times* editor stated that strategic defense would be "highly provocative" to the Soviets, who would be compelled to respond with a "destabilizing new buildup of Soviet offensive weapons." But this argument is porous.[41]

For one, the Soviet Union has been taking steps to develop its own strategic defenses (to an even greater extent than the United States has done or is planning to do) without hearing the charge that their actions are "highly provocative." Another fault is that it is not true that a new Soviet strategic buildup would be justified in response. Such a buildup would only betray a desire on the part of the Soviets to achieve a first-strike capability.

Brzezinski concluded by urging on the West the only "real" arms control worth fighting for:

The objective of each side should be MSS—mutual strategic security. This means that each side is strategically secure—that it knows that a disarming first strike against its opponents would be militarily futile, and that it is confident that a first strike by its opponent would be suicidal. This kind of real arms control offers greater mutual predictability and stability and can enhance mutual security at lower costs than a full-blown race in weapons technology.[42]

Since this policy has not been employed, it is unwise for one side to rush ahead and scrap its nuclear arsenal. Unilateral advantage does not spell security. Nonetheless, generals, statesmen, and whole parties in Europe favor getting rid of Europe's "flexible response" strategy that prevents a nuclear strike.

The real effect of the Soviet missiles and the vast armies poised at the borders of Western Europe is the same as the effect the members of the SLA had on Patty Hearst as they sat guard outside her closet cell with loaded weapons in their hands. The guns do not have to be fired. The missiles cast a shadow of fear across the continent. That shadow accomplishes as much as firing one of those missiles ever could.

By what strategy could the Soviets overtake Europe without fighting a major battle with the West? What policy maker could have postulated such a scenario? Most likely a policy maker who knew that strategists in the West would miss the focus of the Soviet plan.

As the West negotiates with the Soviets, it is important—even vital—to discern the depth and subtlety of Soviet policy. The policy framework of the Soviet strategy has been the policy of détente. The man who conceived of this policy, Leonid Brezhnev, had been an important member of the Soviet leadership since World War II. He was also Khrushchev's most influential adviser and his eventual successor. The roots of détente go back to the early 1960s.

Since the early 1960s, Brezhnev had played a key role in formulating Soviet method and policy. When he was Soviet leader, he defined the centerpiece of his foreign policy: the policy of détente. It is a policy designed for many purposes, but primarily to drive a wedge into the alliance.

# 6

# *Détente*

We make no secret of the fact that we see detente as the way to create some favorable conditions for peaceful socialist and communist construction.[1]

–Leonid Brezhnev

The degree of Leonid Brezhnev's influence on Soviet policy even as early as the 1940s and 1950s is well documented. It was in the course of his long career, a career that moved along ruthlessly from his native Ukraine to the top of the Soviet hierarchy, that he conceived of and finally implemented the policy of détente.

In his work, *The New Class*, Milovan Djilas described the type of psychological makeup that would have enabled Brezhnev to reach his pinnacle of power.[2] "The thirst for power is insatiable and irresistible among communists," he wrote. "Victory in the struggle for power is equal to being raised to a divinity, failure means the deepest mortification and disgrace." This then is the man who came to the West carrying his olive leaf called détente. And the West eagerly grabbed for it.

The reality framework of the West demands that we believe anyone who wants peace. We want to believe in peace so badly that self-deception infiltrates our thinking. We will tell ourselves not what we know is true but what we wish to be true. The terminology of détente fits perfectly into the West's reality framework. The West believes in peace as a goal. Consequently, the West gravitates toward a person or people who claim to be working for peace.

Brezhnev's intentions, even to a people anxious for peaceful coexistence, should have been readily apparent. In addition to using détente as a means to building his own weapons arsenal, his intention was to eliminate, or at least drastically limit, U.S. influence on the NATO countries and thereby undermine the alliance and isolate the United States from her most important allies.

Indicative of this intention were his constant attempts to sign a peace treaty with Germany. Such a treaty would have effectively legitimized Germany's division under the eyes of international law. This would have, in effect, confirmed the division of Europe along existing lines. Once he had accomplished that, the status quo would have been clearly defined and accepted. Then he would have brought Eastern and Western Europe together into a security sphere minus U.S. influence and/or presence.

If he could have been successful, and it is not yet certain to what degree he was successful, the United States would be totally outside of Europe. Then, along with the identification Europe would feel with the Soviets, it would have been almost reflexive to view the United States as the enemy and source of instability in the world. Phase four of the Soviet strategic plan would be accomplished.

Brezhnev would be glad to know, in spite of his inability to sign such a treaty and to enter into an internationally respected pact with Europe that served his purposes, that his policy of détente had been relatively successful in accomplishing the most important part of the equation—isolating U.S. influence from the Western European sphere.

I have pointed out that evidence of this assertion is mounting daily: Europe refused to agree with U.S. calls for a boycott in light of the Soviet invasion of Afghanistan. The prime minister of Italy condemned the United States for its courageous rescue action after the hijacking of the *Achille Lauro*, and even freed Abbas, the principal terrorist. Europe refused to join in with U.S. sanctions against Libya in the wake of recent terrorist attacks in the airports at Rome and Vienna. Europe loudly protested Reagan's decision not to abide by a flawed and violated SALT II treaty. Neil Kinnock protested U.S. nuclear bases in Great Britain and planned to remove the bases and the weaponry if the Labor party won the election in 1988. These instances indicate that U.S. influence is waning but Soviet influence is strong.

The action against the *Achille Lauro* was taken by PLO terrorists, many of whom received their training in the Soviet Union. Also, the terrorist Abbas escaped to Yugoslavia—a country within the Soviet sphere of influence and control. The ties between Libya and the Soviet Union are strong. The training of terrorists in Libya is supported by the Soviet Union, as is the government of Colonel Qaddafi.

European reaction or lack of reaction to these incidents represents a clear pattern of behavior and identification. The bond between the Soviet Union and Europe is strong and growing stronger. This bond can be expected to grow stronger still. At the Reagan–Gorbachev mini-summit the Soviet Union violated the news blackout and made it appear in Europe that the failure to come to any agreement was the United States' fault. This kind of opportunism drives a wider gap between the United States and her European partners.

For Brezhnev the policy of détente had provided the same kind of opportunism. He had limited knowledge of the United States before the Czech crisis in 1968, but after the crisis and as the Soviet Union struggled to achieve strategic parity with the United States, he began to look ahead to prospects of global dominion.

While Brezhnev was estimating what he could realize through détente, the United States was moving in the same direction. President Kennedy had been the first to endorse "relaxed tensions" with the Soviet Union, agreeing to a ban on the testing of nuclear weapons in July 1963. Richard Nixon was highly critical of Kennedy's policies, thinking that the United States' sale of wheat to the Soviets was only harming the cause of freedom. "Why should we pull them out of their trouble and make communism look better?" he asked. He disliked all aspects of Kennedy's détente, because "The bear is always most dangerous when he stands with his arms open in friendship." The spirit of détente seemed to demand from the United States an improper posture, a conciliatory stance toward the Soviet Union with which Nixon felt ill at ease. He suspected the Soviet motivation for grasping so eagerly at policies that promised, among other things, trade, scientific and cultural exchanges, and the general easing of relations that went with détente.

His future foreign-policy adviser, Henry Kissinger, was also skeptical about the worth of détente. He wrote with great perspicacity about the Soviet psyche that sought to use clandestine "peaceful coexistence" as a cover for its more expansionist motives.[3] While détente allowed the Soviets to extend a hand of peace, it freed the other hand to stockpile arms and prepare for confrontation. This kind of insight, based as it was on Soviet history and foreign-policy tactics and strategies, should have been an antidote for hastily embracing a peace agreement with the Soviets. Neither Nixon nor Kissinger looked at détente through rose-colored glasses.

Given their reservations about détente, it would be especially surprising to find them rushing to embrace its principles. Yet this is exactly what they did. The lure of the promise of peace, a promise that was made at a time when the United States was weakened domestically and internationally by its presence in Vietnam, was too strong to resist. Instead of carefully scrutinizing Soviet history, documents, or foreign-policy behavior, the Nixon administration plunged headlong into an understanding. This understanding rested on the basic principles of agreement signed by Brezhnev and Nixon after months of consideration.[4] The principles essentially bound each superpower to respect each other's vital interests. What insured each party's compliance with these principles? Nothing more than a simple faith in reciprocal kindness. Agreement to the principles was considered well worth it. After all, détente would be a welcome relief from the long period of cold war tensions.

If the United States had reasons for seeking détente with the Soviets, the reverse was also true. Brezhnev had a strong incentive to pursue détente. Brezhnev saw two lines of attack. He sought state-to-state relations with Soviet rivals, and at the same time he sought to support national liberation movements.

Another strong incentive for Brezhnev to pursue détente was that economic relations with the West could improve—especially in the area of the flow of Western credits and technology. In this respect, détente benefited the Soviets far more than it did the West.

Détente gave Brezhnev a strong hand to play. Over a period of years, and remember, time is an important ingredient in the development of the identification between hostage and captor, his policy allowed the Soviets to manipulate the level of tension and fear in the world, especially in Europe. The Soviets could raise the level of tensions and induce an utter fear across the map of Europe, reinforcing a feeling of vulnerability. At the same time that they were increasing tension, they could present themselves as peacemakers.

Brezhnev and the Soviets had a masterly plan, the evolution of which led to the most terrible instruments of terror and fear, nuclear weapons. Brezhnev began placing missiles in Eastern Europe and then stopped, calling instead on arms control negotiations.

Why did he place such an emphasis on arms control negotiations when it appeared as though his strategy was to stockpile arms aimed at Europe?

There appear to be two reasons. The first is that by insisting on arms negotiations, the Soviets appear to be on the side of peacemaker.

By heightening tensions and then stepping back, they are creating this positive image that increases the European identification with the Soviets and strengthens the subsequent bond that forms. All the while, they can discredit the position of the United States. Second, because of the wording of the agreements that comprise détente, arms negotiations amount to a means of assisting actual Soviet military policy because they limit the response of the West to the growth of Soviet military power.

Let us look at the principles of agreement. Of the twelve basic principles that were agreed to, here are some that were put to the test. Both superpowers must

- Prevent the development of situations capable of causing a dangerous exacerbation of their relations.
- Do their utmost to avoid military confrontations.
- Recognize that efforts to obtain a unilateral advantage at the expense of the other, directly or indirectly, are inconsistent with these objectives. (This does not specify what constitutes a unilateral advantage. Isn't ideological warfare, spreading propaganda, and supporting national liberation movements part of looking for a unilateral advantage? If so, then why did these activities continue under détente?)
- Have a special obligation . . . to do everything in their power so that conflicts or situations will not arise which would serve to increase international tensions.
- Make no claim for themselves and would not recognize the claims of anyone else to any special rights or advantages in world affairs. They recognize the sovereign equality of all states.[5]

How could anyone have taken these vaguely worded principles seriously? In May of 1972 this writ of détente was taken quite seriously, at least on the U.S.–Israeli side. This "maximal détente" met with its first test in October of 1973 with the Arab attack on Israel.

If these basic principles had been adhered to, the Egyptian–Syrian attack should not have taken place. It was clearly dependent on massive Soviet support; it could not have failed to cause a dangerous strain on U.S.–Soviet relations; it had as its objective a unilateral advantage for the Soviet Union at the expense of the United States; and it clearly increased international tensions. The principles had been violated. After all, Kissinger later said, the United States and the Soviets were "essentially allied to one of the contenders in the area," making a Soviet–U.S. crisis the inevitable result of an Arab–Israeli conflict. If the Soviets had made any effort to abide by the 1972 agreement, they would have avoided the Arab–Israeli military confrontation.

The agreements that comprised the basis for détente were much more limiting to the West than to the Soviets. Brezhnev believed, correctly as it turned out, that the process of arms negotiations at various levels, ultimately leading to a reduction in Western defense efforts, would weaken NATO and other military alliances and lead to greater equity in those areas where superior Western technology had put the Soviets at a disadvantage.

Just how much ground the Soviets made up during the détente era with respect to defense is readily apparent. Between 1970, when SALT I began, and 1977, when the SALT II treaty was being completed, the Soviets increased their number of strategic warheads from 1,400 to 7,900, whereas the United States increased its number from 2,200 to 7,400. Thus the Soviets outproduced the United States by 1,300 warheads during this period of "arms control." While the Soviets were building up, the United States was not increasing its own military expenditures.[6]

In the Soviet Union, détente represented a policy that would not limit its military effectiveness but would limit that of the West. One can only assume what prompted the West to embrace it so enthusiastically. Apparently, the reality framework that the West held along with the years of stress and tension created by the Soviets had taken their toll. Europe wanted to end the horror of living under the shadow of fear that the Soviets had created. Presumably, Nixon's mistake was to assume that by agreeing to détente, he would strengthen the alliance. After all, it was something they all agreed upon.

The degree of Nixon's miscalculation became clear early on. He did recognize correctly the Europeans' desire for détente. But his eagerness to pursue it was like the behavior of a policeman outside a bank robbery/hostage situation who leaves the confrontation because the hostages request that he does. Nixon let down his guard and did not see the psychological motivation for the European desire for détente.

Early on in détente, suspicion grew between the European capitals and Washington. Whenever Washington accused the Soviets of treaty violation, Europe turned to the Soviets as if to ask, Is it so? Naturally, the Soviets answered that it wasn't true.

The Soviet propaganda mills made sure that the Europeans heard clearly what the Soviets wanted them to hear. The Soviets billed Brezhnev's second summit with Nixon as "a history making event serving the peaceful interests of the whole world." In many ways it was. But the deeper intent of this language was to stress continually the myth of the Soviet peacemaker, increasing European identification with the Soviets and strengthening the bond between them.

Meanwhile, the Soviet goals of détente were not peace serving but self-serving. Brezhnev had said during the détente era that there shall be "no peace with imperialists"; détente was for him a new form of class struggle. One of Brezhnev's primary goals at the second summit had been to convince Nixon to underwrite a credit arrangement for exploitation of the Siberian gas and oil deposits, giving the Soviet Union the technology to drill those fields and to help stave off future energy shortages.

That objective was not realized. Nixon refused to go along with Brezhnev. It is interesting to note here that the pipeline to these gas and oil fields brought the first concrete suggestion that Europe had, in fact, succumbed to the Stockholm Syndrome. When the United States later requested that the Europeans refuse to work with the Soviets because of Soviet activity in Poland, the Europeans turned a deaf ear to the United States—evidence that identification with the Soviets, and the consequent denial of U.S. influence and authority, had taken place.

Détente was an effective propaganda tool created by one of the masters of propaganda, Leonid Brezhnev. Whenever Washington accused the Soviets of verifiable treaty violations, the Soviets simply shot back that the United States was engaged in a disinformation campaign to incite a retaliatory reaction and to poison the atmosphere created by détente. They charged the United States with not living up to the spirit of détente. Whose words did Europe believe?

This same criticism was launched against President Reagan when he voiced a view that much of the U.S. body politic agreed with: that détente, from a U.S. perspective, had failed. The policy of détente, this view continued, became a symbol of the United States' lack of will and weakness. Détente did not stop the arms race, and it did not stabilize the balance of power. If this wasn't enough, it appeared that the United States had long been silent about the benefits of détente to the Soviets and the disadvantages to the United States. For his reluctance to revive détente with the Soviets, Reagan became a target of a hate campaign launched by Soviet propaganda. He was seen as a neo-Nazi, a "new Hitler."[7]

Most damaging to the United States, beyond the damage to the alliance as a whole, was that détente helped to slow the growth of U.S. military power, which enabled the Soviets to gain the military advantage that the United States had for so long enjoyed. Détente also dampened U.S. political and military resolve abroad, as was first demonstrated by the U.S. defeat in Vietnam and the U.S. failure to respond in Angola, despite expanding Soviet pressure.

Brezhnev and his colleagues believed that détente, combined with the tremendous growth in Soviet power in the 1970s, actually facilitated a decisive shift in the global relationship between the capitalist and communist camps in favor of the Soviet Union and its allies. A Soviet diplomat boldly proclaimed: "The years in which the United States had the say as to what could be done in the world and what could not are past once and for all. We can no longer tolerate Washington behaving as if it were the umpire of contemporary history."[8]

The blatant and massive invasion of Afghanistan demonstrated the confidence the Soviet Union feels. Under Brezhnev, Moscow had employed proxies many times with increasing success, but the invasion of Afghanistan was the first time since World War II that direct military force has been used to seize territory outside Eastern Europe.

Still, the United States is accused of rupturing the interests of détente.

In spite of the ominous success the Soviets have realized through détente, it has not always been as successful as they had hoped. The United States, while always trying to utilize what was most promising in détente, has consistently resisted that which was most destructive. There have always been those who have been willing to weigh any Soviet move against the backdrop of their larger goals. Many of these people had a voice in their European governments. Consequently, the identification with the Soviets has not been a constant decline. The United States has used its economic strength to bear against violations and, in effect, slow the bonding between Europe and the Soviet Union. An erratic relationship has characterized the contacts between Washington and Europe.

Although identification with the aggressor minimizes the chances of violent behavior, there is a limit to how positive this identification can be. When parties as influential as the German Social Democrats and British Labour move dangerously close to the Soviet wish for a nonnuclear Europe, they risk allowing their captor to be fully armed and themselves to be without a means of adequate defense. I give Western Europeans the benefit of the doubt and claim it is hostage syndrome, not ignorance, that drives them to disarmament.

It is important to realize that détente has its shortcomings from the Soviet point of view. Therein lies some hope for the future. There are cracks in what sometimes appears to be a monolithic foreign policy on the part of the Soviets.

The West, primarily the United States, must continue to negotiate with the Soviet Union. The United States must still influence events to the good. In knowledgeable negotiation, there is hope.

The Reagan administration has moved in the right direction, with its two-track policy of building up arms and then negotiating reductions. After détente drew its last breath with the invasion of Afghanistan in December 1979, the United States adhered to a few propositions that upset the Soviets: The United States was militarily inferior to the Soviet Union; arms control had contributed to this inferiority; and so the best course was to spend.[9] In President Reagan's words, "We've come a long way since the 1970s, when the United States was full of self-deception and neglected its defenses." From now on, he felt, "We must be strong enough to convince any political aggressor that war could bring no benefit, only disaster."

This is much different psychology than the behavioral modification theory of John Watson, applied during the détente era, which rested on the use of positive and negative stimuli to persuade one's opponents. Watson's ideas, although they work in such fields as advertising and public relations, are a failure in international relations. The idea that the Soviets would reform when we punished their "bad" behavior and rewarded their "good" actions was extremely attractive to those endorsing détente. But it didn't work. The springs of Soviet action were personal gain, not peace. By rearming, Reagan ignored Watson and any system of rewards and punishments. Appeasement was no longer the approach.

As a method for slowing U.S. military growth and limiting U.S. influence, as a rationale for massive Soviet military buildup, détente has been an eminently successful program for the Soviets.

The Reagan administration has been the first in many years that has been able to counter the Soviet policy. This is the root of the administration's emphasis on defense. The United States under Reagan is once again rearming and becoming powerful. The United States is once again willing to take its position as the greatest of nations.

Détente has become Europe's "second line of defense" behind nuclear weapons. Professor Melvyn Krauss suggested that Europeans practice détente with the Soviets so that they won't invade Western Europe. The estimated U.S. commitment to NATO over the next ten years will be about $2.2 trillion.[10] The European commitment to détente strengthens as defense grows, for this allows Europe to keep its conventional defense spending low and its welfare spending high. In short, Europe continues its commitment to the détente–welfare state in proportion with U.S. NATO payments.

Krauss argued that the greater a nation's defense dependence, the greater will be its attachment to détente. He cited polls from Germany and France to confirm this relationship. German attachment to détente exceeds French attachment, just as Krauss would expect, since the French use their own military defenses while the West Germans are backed by the United States. The statistics are overwhelming:

- Sixty-six percent of the West Germans and only 30 percent of the French agree that détente should be pursued independently of the military balance.
- Nineteen percent of the West Germans and 62 percent of the French agree that the West should agree on a list of economic sanctions to be used against the Soviet Union in case of such future actions as Afghanistan or Poland.
- Eighty-six percent of the West Germans and 38 percent of the French believe that the West should seek to increase trade with the East to establish a coooperative relationship and thus support the progress of détente in a mutual interest.[11]

From this evidence it seems irrefutable that a preference for détente is the logical outcome of European "free-riding" and not trusting in the U.S. defense commitment to NATO.

Although Europe has taken U.S. missiles, the price to U.S. foreign policy is high: The Reagan administration has little hope that its efforts to lead Europeans to adopt a hard anti-Soviet line will work. NATO countries practice détente with the Soviets because they feel they need to. They trade with and subsidize the Soviets—as they did with the Siberian gas pipeline—because they feel they have to. This action helped the Soviets and gave them additional leverage against the West. The Soviets once benefited from a détente with the United States, and now they continue to benefit from their friendly relations with Western Europe.

Europe doesn't see in the Soviets the same threat the Americans do. Vulnerable and burdened by the past twenty years of stress, Europe seems to have identified with the Soviet's assessment of the situation. Listen to the words of Egon Bahr, a disarmament expert for the West German Social Democratic party: "In the entire post-war period, we have lived with the threat from the Soviet Union. What is now new is that peace could be threatened by our principle ally—the United States."[12]

In Bahr's statement it is possible to hear some of the echoes of Patricia Hearst's statement to her parents regarding the danger posed to her by the police and the FBI. Bahr has identified the United States as the threat to stability and peace.

The process of humanization through positive contacts (or the absence of negative ones) between the hostage and the captor induces those hostage syndrome traits. It is, therefore, not on whim that Soviet leaders frequent European capitals. During Brezhnev's visit to West Germany in 1981, the demonstrators were loudly protesting nonexistent U.S. missiles and shouting anti-Reagan rhetoric; they were silent about the SS-20s and Brezhnev's strong-arm Eastern European policy.

Détente has allowed the Soviets to distort European perceptions of the Soviet intentions and of the world. Once again, as evidence of the hostage syndrome trait of hating and fearing the police, we examine the words of Dorothee Solle: "Evil has an address, a telephone number. You can name it. We know who liquidated Hiroshima, not to mention Nagasaki. We can point out the American Senators who are for arming and earn dividends on it."[13]

The Soviets have caused an about face in the way Europe perceives them.

In this context, Mikhail Gorbachev becomes even more frightening. His leadership is highly stylized, and its intent is to woo the leaders of Western Europe into believing that the failure of arms control owes to the United States. Even Mrs. Thatcher, a strong Reagan supporter, delighted in his visit. She felt they could "do business." With the breaking down of negotiations in Reykjavik and the increasing popularity of opposition parties in Western Europe, we can expect much more "business" between Gorbachev and our allies.

# 7

# *Mikhail Gorbachev*

A serious threat is hovering over European culture. The threat emanates from an onslaught of "mass culture" from across the Atlantic. We understand pretty well the concerns of West European intellectuals. Indeed one can only wonder why a deep, profoundly intelligent and inherently humane European culture is retreating to the background before the primitive revelry of violence and pornography and the flood of cheap feelings and low thoughts.

Mikhail Gorbachev, Perestroika

Mikhail Gorbachev, protégé of Yuri Andropov. The same Yuri Andropov who was head of the Soviet Secret Police and Intelligence Agency, the KGB. Mikhail Gorbachev has picked up the thread of the modern Soviet legacy—the thread that leads back to Nikita Khrushchev. Mikhail Gorbachev came to leadership of the Soviet Union and immediately pressed for the continuation of détente. In this respect he has the same yearnings as his predecessors.

In the words of the Sovietologist Professor Seweryn Bialer, "Gorbachev will in all probability be regarded as one of the major reformers in Russian history."[1] Others also feel that Gorbachev will be a strong leader and will attempt to transform systematically the Soviet economic system. Still others think that Gorbachev may only be interested in cosmetic changes—such as enforcing discipline in the work place and combating alcoholism among workers. Critics point out that his speeches and discussions betray a general failure to penetrate the deeper causes of the economic problems in the Soviet Union. It is sometimes noted that Gorbachev's harsh critiques of domestic life in the Soviet Union are coupled with feeble remedial policies to effect change. As Marshall Shulman wrote in *Foreign Affairs*, "One must be agnostic on Gorbachev's chances of success with the problems he faces."[2]

There is more than a little cause for agnosticism. It is widely thought that if Gorbachev aims for a fundamental reform of the Soviet system, he may lose respect in the Politburo, especially among hardliners who are resistant to change. There is conservative opposition throughout the Soviet system. Indeed, 60 percent of all voting members of the 307-member Central Committee are holdovers from the Brezhnev era, unlikely to be enthusiastic about Gorbachev's de-Brezhnevization campaigns.[3] Faced with legions of neo-Stalinist defenders of the status quo, Gorbachev doesn't have the kind of autonomy he needs to make certain changes.[4] Like other Soviet policy makers, Gorbachev knows what is wrong with the economy. The problems are not just economical. When Gorbachev took office, there were widespread alcoholism, poor work ethics, low living standards, inferior health care, a low birth rate, a high divorce rate, massive waste of natural resources, ruthless despoliations of the environment, and ubiquitous corruption.[5] Moreover, as Richard Nixon pointed out, Gorbachev must face the classic dilemma of communist totalitarian systems: To have progress, he must allow more freedom. Allowing more freedom, however, threatens his power, for centralized authority is the sine qua non of the communist system.[6]

Gorbachev has embarked on *perestroika* or restructuring, of the Soviet economy, moving in the direction of less centralization and planning, more initiative at the work place, and more respect for market forces. He has pushed such aspects of perestroika as *glasnost* (openess), *demokratizatsia* (democratization), and "new thinking."

To be sure, glasnost is not equivalent to freedom of the press. Vladislov Krasnov, a Soviet historian, wrote: "Glasnost abolishes neither censorship nor Party caution. But under Glasnost one can begin to describe reality as it is. One can even criticize that reality as long as the holy cows of Socialism, Communism, Lenin, the October Revolution, and the Party remain untouched." Krasnov then offered a sample of revelations that now fill the pages of Soviet publications:

According to an article published last year, official Soviet statistics are utterly unreliable. For example, while official Soviet statistics say that the national income during the 1928–85 period grew 90 times, the authors estimate the growth at only six to seven times. Notice the discrepancy: it is not ten or even a hundred percent, but about 13 times! . . .

My colleague at Hoover, Mikhail Bernstan, estimates that "about 40 percent of the Soviet people live below the Soviet poverty line, which is itself about one-third lower than the U.S. poverty line." Other statistics show falsifications of the infant mortality rate.[7]

If Gorbachev continues to go after major reforms, he is likely to meet the kind of opposition that Khrushchev encountered. Khrushchev was eventually removed from office because of his strong anti-Stalinism. Like Khrushchev, Gorbachev is up against an old guard of conservatives. After negotiating the reduction and eventual elimination of intermediate nuclear forces (INF) in Europe, Gorbachev addressed people on television and was skeptical about whether the Supreme Soviet or the U.S. Senate would ratify the INF treaty. There was a depressed tone in his voice, in contrast to all the media ballyhoo surrounding the Washington summit. "People constantly ask me how matters proceeded at the Summit. It's too early to say if there's a fundamental improvement or a turning point in Soviet–American relations," Gorbachev said.[8] Television commentator Vladimir Posner told the Soviet people that the Soviets are giving up four times as many weapons as the United States. The impression given was one of an unequal treaty with far too many Soviet concessions.[9]

Despite opposition at home and an adversarial administration in Washington, Gorbachev remains a new kind of leader for the Kremlin. He is new in style and substance. If Gorbachev has his way, both domestic policy and foreign policy in the Soviet Union will undergo radical changes. Internally, Soviet output might be increased by decentralizing authority. He realizes the need to provide farmers, workers, and foremen with greater incentives. As evidenced by his critiques, he is the first Soviet leader to admit to basic problems that threaten the Soviet Union's status as a superpower.

Gorbachev's ideas about democratization call for many changes:

- greater democracy in the selection of party officials;
- secret ballots;
- competition among two or more candidates;
- broader criticism in Soviet television, journals, plays, and movies to an extent most Americans would have thought impossible;
- criticism of party corruption;
- questioning privileges of the party elite;
- cutting down abuses of the KGB.

His speeches, however, have reflected concern with the party that freer criticism might lead to anarchy.[10]

Gorbachev needs a break in military spending to carry out some of his reforms at home. However, if he doesn't get this break, one should not assume that further military expenses will cause the Soviet edifice to topple. Creating external pressure has long been a practice of U.S. foreign policy, but it doesn't always succeed. For the economic well-being of the Soviet Union, Gorbachev wants to reduce heavy military spending, which has gone above 16 percent of the Soviet GNP. Thus, at Reykjavik, when Reagan refused to back off the costly Star Wars effort, Gorbachev saw that he was in trouble and boasted, "I know there are people in your country who would like to spend us out of existence. We will not let this happen."[11]

Instead of accepting inequalities in military spending, he said he would do something he did not want to do: lower living standards in order to compete. There again is evidence of the Soviet's old guard.

Much of what Gorbachev stands for seems to thrust at the very heart of the Soviet system. In pushing for outside economic aid, for instance, he ignores the Soviet Union's historically closed borders; in backing local leader's demands for greater autonomy, he flies in the face of the Soviets' cherished central planning.

Under Gorbachev the Soviets have also displayed an eagerness and flexibility in reaching arms accords that Western analysts see as unprecedented in the history of postwar Soviet arms proposals. He personally rejected the "walkout" position of November 1983, when Moscow refused the Pershing II and cruise missiles that Americans had deployed on European soil. Despite this "new" stance, he objected to Reagan's tenacious hold on Star Wars at Reykjavik. Nonetheless, despite initial attacks on U.S. insincerity at the negotiating table, he looked forward to possible progress at the Washington summit in December 1987.

It is here that Gorbachev shines brightly. With arms negotiations and their publicized aftermath, Gorbachev brings all his powers to bear. Stylish leader, tireless worker, new thinker, motivated reformer—Gorbachev summons all these attributes during periods of contact with the West. To appreciate the force of Gorbachev's person and philosophy, it is instructive to look at some of his major concerns.

Gorbachev's overarching philosophy about nuclear weapons is that they should be eliminated. He is an abolitionist. This is, of course, a far cry from just saying that armaments should be reduced. "If there's to be life," he argued, "nuclear weapons must cease to be."[12] Just as we deprive children of matches, Gorbachev believes we must deprive leaders of weapons before they incinerate our home. It's his pursuit of this end that allows Gorbachev to shine—in the United States and Europe. He's impatient when negotiations stall on numbers and kinds of weapons. When this impatience grows, he finds fault with those providing the obstacles and relentlessly pursues solutions.

When the United States was hesitant to accept his moratorium on the testing of nuclear weapons and later his Reykjavik "zero option," he scored propaganda victories with NATO allies. When Europeans desired to keep a nuclear deterrent, he bristled over Western leaders' "stone age ways of thinking." He has cast his nuclear position into a frightful either/or: You either side with me and abolish these damnable weapons, or we will all one day suffer nuclear annihilation. Nixon believes him, but only to a point. He wrote: "He doesn't want war. But he just as sincerely wants victory without war. . . . He has continued to preserve the long-term objective of global predominance, despite the refinements he's introduced into Moscow's public relations techniques."[13]

Not five months after the frustration of Reykjavik, Gorbachev accepted the formerly unacceptable zero option, a plan to eliminate U.S. and Soviet medium-range weapons in Europe without touching the French and British forces.[14] In September 1987 it was announced in *Pravda* that Gorbachev had suggested an accord with the United States to cut strategic weapons by 50 percent.[15] By one count Gorbachev has already made more than twenty-five distinct arms control moves in his first two years as Soviet general secretary.[16] All of these moves were unreciprocated by the Reagan administration. But the Washington summit changed that.

In Washington the two leaders struck a deal that is singular in the nuclear age. An entire class of weapons will be eliminated if Congress should ratify the treaty. The INF treaty proposes to destroy all intermediate-range missiles (600 to 3,300 miles), all short-range missiles (300 to 600 miles), and their associated launchers, support facilities, and bases. If fully implemented, the Soviets will scrap 1,836 missiles; the United States, 859. On the surface, the treaty looks favorable to the United States and NATO. But opinion is mixed on just how beneficial the treaty will be for the defense of Western Europe. "Those missiles," said Joseph Nye, Jr., director of Harvard University's Center for Science and International Relations, "were put there for political reasons." NATO wanted them as a demonstration of the U.S. resolve to defend them. "Their removal has to be judged by the same standards."[17] The argument may be a cogent one: What essential components of NATO's defense plans have changed to make the missiles unnecessary? The best answer seems to be none. But it has long been Gorbachev's desire to see a nuclear-free Europe.

Admiral William J. Crowe, Jr., chairman of the joint chiefs of staff, feels that the treaty changes little militarily. He told the Senate Armed Services Committee during the initial ratification hearings: "If the West can keep its arms reduction policy consistent with the NATO strategy of flexible response, we can maintain the security we seek at reasonable levels of investment—not to mention reducing the risk of nuclear devastation. The treaty has no impact on NATO's fundamental strategy."[18] Jack N. Merritt, a retired army general who served on the alliance's Military Committee, agreed: "I wouldn't make too much of the treaty's benefits or risks. It's probably beneficial at the margins. It removes the missile threat to NATO ports and airfields. We lose something with the flexibility and accuracy of the Pershings. But on balance it's probably positive."[19]

But there is hardly universal agreement on the deal that Gorbachev wanted so badly. Edward N. Luttwak, the senior fellow at the Center for Strategic and International Studies, dislikes the treaty, despite its move toward arms reductions. Luttwak called the deal

a political necessity and a piece of strategic recklessness of rare dimensions. We surrender the weapons designed to deter a conventional invasion of Europe in exchange for weapons for which Soviet strategy has no current use. The SS-20 lost all military utility when the Soviets developed (in the 1970s) a non-nuclear war-winning capability. It isn't Pershings against the SS-20s. It's Pershings and Cruises against the Soviet army. The Pershing is the only weapon we have capable of taking out those superhardened Soviet command centers."

These command centers are the underground complexes built to withstand intense conventional bombings and nuclear near-misses, at least from smaller bombs.[20]

If the deal was a poor one from the standpoint of NATO's defense needs, as Nye and Luttwak asserted, then it is more than a little impressive that Gorbachev could get the United States to sign away a crucial part of Europe's deterrent. Gorbachev has a way of making people identify with him.

The cornerstone of Stockholm Syndrome, it should be recalled, is identification with the captor. The identification with Gorbachev has already been extensive. Considering his apparent honesty, his dynamism as a leader, and Europe's diminished confidence in Reagan, Gorbachev has definitely opened the door to further dealings with Europe. Nixon suggested that "Gorbachev's neatly tailored suits, refined manners, beautiful wife and smooth talk with reporters have made him a star with the press and diplomatic corps."[21] A U.S. official even remarked on his "good eye contact, firm handshake and deep, melodious voice." A British politician went further, noting that "Gorbachev is the most admired man in the world."[22] A disarmament expert further escalated the admiration saying, "Gorbachev is like Jesus. He just keeps giving out good things, like arms control proposals."[23]

Despite this adulation, one analyst described the most recent summit as "the week Washington lost its head."[24] Georgi Arbatov surmised, "Gorbachev's secret weapon is to deprive America of the enemy." Indeed, this is a summation of Gorbachev's prolonged message in Washington: We're not enemies, but brothers and neighbors, toughing it out against the scourges of the planet, especially nuclear weapons. The only cure for this last scourge, as the Soviet general secretary sees it, is total abolition, nuclear idealism to the highest power. He has proposed total disarmament by the year 2000.

To achieve this end, he desires a return to détente. In his book *Perestroika*, he described his plans for Europe: "I thought for a long time and settled on the metaphor, 'Europe is our common home.' . . . I felt with growing acuteness the artificiality and temporariness of the bloc-to-bloc confrontation."[25] He desires a Europe that is "safer" and free of the possibility of "a nuclear conflagration."

His "design" for Europe leads him to chastise Europeans for allowing the United States to fly through European air space to bomb Libya. "This reminded me of the appeasement of aggressors in World War II."[26] Evidently, hyperbole and false analogies are not alien to Gorbachev's arsenal. He cannot understand how NATO nations can be stricken with panic over the zero option.[27] To those who have reminded him of Western Europe's need to arm against the ominous might of the Warsaw Pact nations, he has responded, "The West was the first to set up a military alliance."[28] "The Warsaw Pact Treaty," he explained, "was signed after the establishment of NATO."[29] This, of course, seems deliberately antihistorical; the NATO alliance was formed out of fear, fear of a further Soviet advance into Europe. Gorbachev concluded that both nations should eliminate their military alliances. Hearing Gorbachev talk this way and by construing his actions as moving toward a goal of total disarmament within the next fifteen years, some are sure that he intends to divide the United States from her Atlantic ally. What better way to accomplish this than by proposals that move NATO toward the zero option?

It may be true that U.S. policy makers' thinking about the Soviet Union became utterly militarized under Reagan.[30] It may also be true that European confidence in the United States has been undermined by words and deeds of the Reagan administration. Early on, Reagan talked of limited nuclear war and the possibility of "escalation dominance" in a military conflict to get the Soviets to accommodate us.[31] Then the president planned to undercut four decades of military strategy in Europe with his talk of a space shield over the United States, not over Europe.[32] At Reykjavik the Europeans watched as Reagan came perilously close to an agreement to eliminate all nuclear missiles in Europe, without previous warning. Despite these setbacks, keeping a sharp watch on armaments negotiations is of paramount importance.

Treating arms reduction talks as though they were an end in themselves, however, rather than as a means to Atlantic security, can be extremely dangerous. Some argue that NATO has already been wounded by the INF agreement, as we have noted. Therefore, what looks to many like a prudent deal is on closer inspection a bad deal when one considers that the intermediate-range weapons that we are trading are the most powerful in Europe and the only ones capable of striking Soviet targets from the European theater.[33] Without the sophisticated cruises and the Pershings, Europe has nearly 8,000 weapons, but very few intermediate-range warheads. The moral for this and future agreements is clear: Negotiations to reduce nuclear weaponry must serve as a means to an end; an imprudent deal is inferior to no deal at all.

It is especially important that the West not let itself be led astray by the "charm offensive" of the new Soviet leader. With degrees in agronomy and law, Gorbachev has an unusual background and may be the best-educated Soviet leader in a very long time. The terms he used to couch his proposals, as well as his overall mob appeal, create new possibilities for the Soviet Union. One analyst even pointed out that the language used to describe him is the kind usually reserved for St. George rather than a Communist party leader.[34] Charles Krauthammer pointed out that Gorbachev makes palpable the fallacy that the two superpowers are morally equivalent.[35] When Gorbachev claims that "no technological solutions to security exist"—that security can only be mutual—we would do well to keep in mind how different the two nations' goals are and whether there can be changes in the political structure of the world that both sides would regard as beneficial.

The United States should, indeed must, come to the negotiating table. But not without preconditions.

The United States should recognize what is happening in Europe with regard to the Soviets. We can expect that Gorbachev will meet personally with European leaders, as he did in 1985, in order to "do business." If U.S.-Soviet relations resemble the cold war period of several decades ago, we can expect that the Soviets will negotiate with Europe rather than the United States. The Euro-Soviet bond continues to grow stronger as Europeans become more disenchanted with U.S. leadership.

The Soviets have been manipulating world events and the tension of world politics to reach this end. Gorbachev has brought the Europeans closer to the view that the United States blocks the road to international harmony, that the United States is impossible to deal with, and that world safety can be attained without it.

# 8

# *Ten Recommendations*

What should U.S. policy be? Let's look at ten recommendations for NATO.

## 1.  WITHDRAWAL?

Some of the most prominent voices in the West are calling for partial or total withdrawal of U.S. military commitment to NATO. Sam Nunn, Henry Kissinger, Zbigniew Brzezinski, and Melvyn Krauss are just a few of the distinguished persons who desire that the present NATO arrangement be fundamentally changed.[1] Since NATO has existed for the sake of European security, a withdrawal of U.S. troops from NATO would be tantamount to scrapping the thirty-nine-year-old treaty between the United States and her allies. If the military portion of the relationship were removed, would European–U.S. relations still exist?

Probably. Europe and the United States share important interests other than a defense against the Soviet Union. They share such Western values as human rights, liberal government, and a desire to be free from tyranny. Therefore, to conclude automatically that a U.S. military withdrawal would lead Europe to seek cozier relations with the Soviets is hasty. Europe has much to fight for, with or without the United States.

They also have the raw potential to oppose the Soviet Union. As Melvyn Krauss has pointed out, "There is nothing inherent in the military inferiority of Western Europe. They have three times the GNP of the Soviets, four times the population and technical superiority.''[2] Moreover, Western Europe has no analogue to Moscow's problems with its captive East European states.

Still, there are risks inherent in a U.S. withdrawal of nuclear bases from Western Europe. If the United States were to satisfy the wishes of the peace movement and left-of-center European parties by packing up and leaving behind a nonnuclear Europe, all of Western Europe would be susceptible to the following threats:

The Soviets possess superior conventional forces, so any uncalculated withdrawal would leave Europe extremely vulnerable to Soviet and Warsaw Pact forces. This would be true even while Europe would be undergoing a strategic transition from nuclear to conventional forces. European conventional forces would have to be strengthened and already in place. Even then the risks would be profound.[3]

A purely conventional defense in Europe, contrary to what many are saying, should only take effect when the Soviets have relinquished all their INFs targeted on our allies. Without the fulfillment of this condition Europe would be setting itself up for political pressure from the Soviets. Instead of being secure, the continent would be subject to nuclear blackmail and attack. It is the height of military irresponsibility to deny this and allow an opening for the Soviets to do what they have long desired to do. Moreover, even an East–West agreement to abolish all intermediate-range nuclear forces would be irresponsible. Later in this chapter I shall show why a nuclear-free Europe is highly undesirable.

A policy of U.S. withdrawal, even a phased five-year withdrawal of the sort Kissinger and others advocate, should only be adopted if certain conditions are obtained.[4] The most important prerequisite would be leaving behind a nuclear deterrent in rough parity with the Soviets' INFs. Kissinger even suggested that we give Western Europe our nuclear weapons gratis. This would allow his full plan to unfold. Since "existing arrangements [with Europe] are unbalanced," said Kissinger, and since nuclear weapons are the "real deterrent to any kind of attack," the United States could withdraw up to half of its present ground forces.

In short, U.S. withdrawal from Europe is not unthinkable, as some would have us believe. But just any U.S. withdrawal that would leave Europe a sitting duck is unwise.

## 2. "THE TAIL WAGGING THE DOG"

Although a withdrawal of U.S. troops and weaponry is probably too severe a measure for many in Washington, they would have to admit that the present NATO situation is not satisfactory either. After all, the present NATO relationship, to quote Krauss, is one in which "the tail wags the dog."[5] Theodore Draper drew a similar conclusion: The Atlantic alliance may be the only one in history in which the ruling partner receives less from the subject than the subject does from the ruling partner.[6] Without a doubt the United States appeases her allies, as if appeasement were a bona fide policy.

European leaders are very aware of the leverage they have over Washington. They will continue to exert this leverage until the responsibilities to Euro-defense are altered. No incentives presently exist for Europe to be strong against the Soviet Union or to follow any of the United States' foreign policy directives. The system of responsibilities in NATO gives them no incentives. Nor does the United States seek to reverse the tables and gain leverage on the Europeans by using fear. Krauss aptly described the NATO relationship:

Europe has leverage over the United States. So long as the United States insists on defending Europe, our allies can use the "you-do-as-we-say-or-we-don't-let-you-defend-us" threat against us. But why, Americans may ask, do we insist on defending the Europeans and thus give them the leverage they use so well by manipulating United States policies? Wouldn't it be better if we simply dealt with the Europeans on a take-it-or-leave-it basis? If the Europeans really don't want to be protected by us, why humiliate ourselves by foisting United States protection on them? Moreover, forcing "free-goods" like nuclear protection down the throats of our allies can only strengthen anti-American neutralist and pacifist elements in allied countries.[7]

To Krauss, the best remedy is withdrawal of U.S. troops and nuclear commitments from Europe. I part company with Krauss when he says the Soviets don't necessarily desire a split in the Atlantic alliance, because they wouldn't wish to contend with the United Europe—a potential third superpower in the world. As I have already pointed out, there is vast evidence to show that the Soviets desire to divide the alliance. Krauss construed this evidence in a clever way:

The theory that the objective of the U.S.S.R. is to split the United States from the rest of the Atlantic alliance is the most important lever the Europeans currently have over United States foreign policy. . . . To deny the U.S.S.R. its victory, Atlantic unity has been made the sine qua non of United States foreign policy. If the United States protests Europe's policies, the doctrine of Atlantic unity is waved in America's face.[8]

Instead of being upset at the allies for free-riding and being irresponsible toward the alliance and friendly with the Soviets, we should blame the system that allows them to take U.S. defense commitments and be ingrates at the same time. The Atlantic unity doctrine absurdly says that no matter how our allies behave, we must not cross them.

We must create incentives for our allies, and these incentives must result in a change of attitude on their part. Americans complain that Europeans shirk their duties to NATO, but we encourage them to. In this vein Krauss concluded, "Nations like individuals respond to incentives. When the United States gave Europe a defense guarantee, it also gave the Europeans an incentive to minimize their own defense efforts. . . . To engage European behavior, Washington must change the incentive structure faced by our allies."[9] The United States must provide less to defend Europe, and Europe must provide more.

### 3.  "TAKE IT OR LEAVE IT?"

What then could be done to change the incentive structure in NATO? What can be done to change the leverage that Europe now has? The United States should demand Europe's compliance and lead the alliance instead of just "taking what it can get."

U.S. leverage, of course, lies in the $165 billion they spend on Europe each year (and an estimated $2.2 trillion over the next ten years[10]), which in turn allows Europe to divert great sums of money to their welfare states. Even if Europe began to comply regularly with U.S. wishes, some say the price is still too high. Why should the United States help Europe by writing them a blank check for defense if Europe won't help itself?

Some suggest that Europe will "Finlandize" itself if the United States cuts NATO spending. Some statesmen feel that the West's number one threat today is not a Soviet invasion of Europe, but a systematic accommodation to Soviet policies on the part of Europe. But as Western Europe becomes further neutralized, the United States accommodates its allies to a great degree. Krauss pointed out that even the Reagan administration has given up on its efforts to get Europe to adopt a tough anti-Soviet line. Instead, the administration has adopted the chief European concerns: détente, summitry, and arms control.[11]

Why must the United States be pressured to order their policies to fit European demands? Europeans complain about the belligerence of U.S. policy, its brash optimism, and bold actions. But Reagan has on several occasions resisted the opportunity to threaten Europe. He could have threatened Europe with punishments when they subsidized the Soviet gas pipeline. Perhaps the time has come for the United States to take action, to boldly lead Europe instead of going where the European mood leads them.

A solution to the problems of the NATO alliance was proposed by David Calleo.[12] Calleo argued that the alliance is an economic, political, and military disaster. What to do? Calleo repeatedly made use of two concepts in his solution—hegemony and devolution.

The United States seeks a postwar pax Americana, hegemony over Europe. But it should let this desire go. Rather it should devolve, that is, transfer military and political power to the alliance, creating a more "Europeanized" Europe. Rather than being a sole authority in the alliance, the United States should compromise, letting go some of the control it now has without surrendering complete sovereignty.

The United States' role in NATO should change from protector to ally. Increasing resentment exists for Europe's free-riding on U.S. defense spending. From Europe's standpoint, the protectorate is preferable. Why shouldn't they want their military problems handled from across the Atlantic? It's cheap and leaves them free for other matters. Indeed, 58 percent of the United States' overall defense spending goes toward NATO.[13]

Traditionally, the NATO allies have resisted the U.S. pressure to take on a greater share of the defense burden. Germany spends 3.3 percent of its GNP on defense; France, 4.1 percent; Britain, 5.5 percent; and the United States, 6.4 percent.[14] NATO governments spend less than they can for their conventional and nuclear defense.

NATO, therefore, represents an oversized military commitment for the United States. This commitment is a major contributor to the United States' desperate fiscal crisis. While Europeans have been militarily undeveloped, the United States has been militarily overextended as a result. Devolution, not hegemony, seems the best policy.

None of the counterarguments to a policy of devolution are convincing. First, it is said that Europeans are incapable of organizing themselves to cooperate. Second, the Soviets are said to be too great a political threat or economic attraction. However, the combined wealth and technology of NATO governments is far in excess of that of the Soviet Union and her allies. Moreover, it is unlikely with Europe's present anticommunist leadership that the Soviet Union appears economically or politically attractive.

Calleo's devolution solution can be carried out by U.S. leaders. The United States must not look at the world as bipolar. Both liberals and conservatives are in a bipolar time warp, one side favoring arms control, the other an arms race. The United States must accept the reality that it is not really supreme. What is needed is a more indigenous European defense. The United States can no longer sustain a large land army for Europe: It is politically and economically unrealistic.

An end to U.S. hegemony seems the most realistic policy. Drastic measures, such as an end to U.S. participation in Europe's defense or ending the NATO treaty, are not needed. Devolution implies handing over some of the authority and responsibility to NATO governments, nothing more.

With respect to the Atlantic alliance, there is little reason for the United States to "take it or leave it."

## 4.  EUROPE'S INSECURITIES

Although there is little reason to suffer a "take it or leave it" attitude from NATO governments, the United States should be aware of Europeans' insecurities. For instance, when we negotiate major arms deals behind their backs, as we did at Reykjavik, this can only damage any chances of mutual cooperation. If we decide to make decisions of global importance, we should let European leaders in on them. They should not have had to learn after the Reagan–Gorbachev meeting that by 1991 they may not have any thermonuclear weaponry. A decision like this is crucial to their security.

Because of decisions such as this, many Europeans get the insecure feeling that the East–West struggle goes on over their heads. They feel that a third world war might be fought on their state without them having any say.

We should give them less reason to worry. Several actions of the Reagan administration have strained the Atlantic alliance and given rise to fears in Europe. The last two summit meetings have perplexed and worried European leaders. In particular, a process of "denuclearization" has been set in motion. The bombing of Libya and the Iran–contra scandal, in addition to defense issues, have reduced European confidence in U.S. leadership.

Consider Reykjavik first. Had it not been for Reagan's firm adherence to Star Wars, Europe would be defending its soil without nuclear weaponry. Mikhail Gorbachev's proposal called for, among other things, all Soviet and U.S. medium-range (300 to 3,000 miles) missiles to be removed from Europe. But before this move went through, Gorbachev wanted Reagan's word that testing and research on the Strategic Defense Initiative (SDI) would be stopped.

Reductions talks went a little too far to suit the tastes of NATO governments. Admiral Sir James Eberle of the British royal navy expressed the view of many European government and military officials in an interview after Reykjavik.[15] The admiral, who was NATO commander in chief for the eastern Atlantic fleet and retired from the active list of the royal navy in 1983, said "a world rid of nuclear weapons is less stable." Thus, "deterrence is undermined by the President's conviction." This conviction is Reagan's quest for a space-based defense against nuclear weapons. Whatever the other shortcomings of SDI, it does, as the admiral pointed out, undercut the military strategy of deterrence that the United States has adhered to for four decades.

The NATO guarantee, also in place for four decades, was also threatened by the negotiations in Iceland. "Europeans now ask," said Admiral Eberle, "are those (alliance) guarantees we have been operating under really worth anything?" In startling contrast to the postwar cold war years, U.S. leadership is now questioned and widely mistrusted. The criticism from the standpoint of European interests is not unfounded.

Europe's insecurity over U.S. commitment may have been born with de Gaulle's withdrawal from the protection of the nuclear umbrella. De Gaulle doubted that the United States would risk its own annihilation, as promised by the NATO treaty, if war came to Europe. The fear of the "decoupling" of the United States and Europe in the event of a crisis was increased after a speech delivered by Henry Kissinger in 1977. Kissinger warned that the United States might not necessarily be willing to respond with its strategic nuclear force to a limited Soviet military war in Europe.[16] This led to a campaign about the danger of the decoupling of the U.S. strategic nuclear deterrent from the European theater. In turn, this led to a campaign, headed by the then West German Chancellor Helmut Schmidt, to get cruise and Pershing II intermediate-range missiles in Europe, in response to the Soviet SS-20s.

What was planned in Reykjavik was agreed upon during the December 1987 summit in Washington. The INF treaty, signed by President Reagan and Mikhail Gorbachev and ratified by the Senate in April 1988, will lead to the destruction of the Pershings and cruises that Europe wanted less than a decade ago. These INF missiles were a response to the SS-20s but also a symbol of the U.S. political commitment to defend Western Europe. Others argued that the missiles would fill a gap in NATO's land-based long-range nuclear capabilities and thereby serve the goals of the NATO strategy of "flexible response" if a crisis demanded a threat of escalation. U.S. strategists were attracted to the flexibility of these missiles, too.

The Reagan administration first proposed the zero option in 1981. Mikhail Gorbachev sees the option and thus the INF agreement as enhancement for his political stature. But reigning NATO leaders think nuclear deterrence is safer than conventional deterrence. To them, the possibility of nuclear war is far less likely with nuclear deterrence than without it. First, there were members of the Reagan administration who thought that "victory" in a nuclear war was possible. Now the same administration seeks to eliminate a crucial part of NATO's nuclear defense against the East.

No wonder that European leaders are insecure about the decisions made in Washington.

## 5.  TRIUMPH OVER ATTITUDES

Attitudes expressing fatalism or defeatism must be banished. "Better red than dead" is still embraced by some who feel that the only two alternatives in today's world are a meek, accommodating policy toward the Soviets or death by nuclear devastation. But survival-is-enough types are missing a fundamental point. If survival involves no more than life on the Gulag or Soviet occupation of one's country, it has little value. What has value is a life in which Western values and ideals are preserved. To preserve these, strength must remain our policy.

Jonathan Schell and Mikhail Gorbachev are perhaps the two most prominent figures to embrace the total abolition of atomic weapons. In two well-known works, *The Fate of the Earth* and *The Abolition*, Schell argued for the complete elimination of weapons, which will result in a more secure world.[17] Gorbachev desires to rid the world of weapons by the year 2000.[18] Both men say that abolition is morally preferable to having any missiles lying around. But this conclusion is valid only if nuclear abolition best ensures survival. Schell argued that under abolition the two chief causes for a nuclear holocaust are absent: a preemptive strike by one of the superpowers and a nuclear accident leading to war. But Schell's empirical argument fails to convince. Surely, it is possible—perhaps even likely—that if two nations are disarmed, one could then arm rapidly and have its way with the other. Schell counters by claiming that a secretive first strike is "unlikely," but his claim rests on nothing more secure than possibility, trust, faith, or goodwill. Would you rather that your national security rested on strategic deterrence or the good will of the Soviets?

On the day of his election Gorbachev spoke on arms control: "We need an agreement which would help all to advance toward the cherished goal: the complete elimination and prohibition for all times, toward the complete removal of the threat of nuclear war. This is our firm conviction."[19] Yet, if the goal of nations is survival, and the probability of that goal increases under strategic stability, then Gorbachev's option is immoral for not being the one that serves the end of survival. Instability comes from inequality of forces, and no greater chance for nuclear advantage occurs than under a condition of disarmament.

Such strategic plans as unilateral disarmament (to decrease the payload or destructive power of the world's weapon total) and abolition of atomic weapons are ill conceived. Worse, they are dangerous. Both of these approaches are really dressed up versions of "better red than dead." Both are cowardly policies and concede more to world security than is necessary or rational. Instead of meeting the strategic challenge head on, disarmament and abolition are fatalistic twins. They recommend adopting a policy without will, as if strength of will didn't matter.

If fatalism represents a poor philosophy in East–West relations, defeatism and belligerence are poorer cousins. "Worse case analyses" that place "the enemy" on a pedestal of invincible evil get us nowhere. Using the worst-case scenario as a basis for strategic policy only fuels the arms buildup. The fallacy of getting into an arms race posture is that one side thinks it can gain a lead and eventually win.

Robert McNamara, secretary of defense under President Kennedy, told us how damaging misrepresentation can be. The sober-minded McNamara claimed he "has never heard a Senior U.S. Military Officer express any doubt whatsoever about our ability to penetrate Soviet air space."[20] He pointed out that in 1985 Lawrence Gershwin of the Central Intelligence Agency testified before Congress that "against a combined attack of penetrating bombers and Cruise missiles, Soviet air defenses during the next ten years probably would be incapable of inflicting sufficient losses to prevent large-scale damage to the U.S.S.R."[21] Add to this that no less than the joint chiefs of staff stated they would not trade forces—both offensive and defensive—with the Soviets. "General David Jones, former Chairman of the Joint Chiefs of Staff, said in 1980, 'I would not swap our present military capability with that of the Soviet Union.' ''[22] Furthermore, the current joint chiefs of staff chairman, Admiral William Crowe, testified on February 5, 1986, that there was "rough parity" between the United States and the Soviet Union.

So what did the Reagan administration do upon first taking office? Essentially, they lied. They warned of a "window of vulnerability"[23]—the danger that land-based U.S. missiles could be destroyed in their silos by a surprise Soviet attack. The improbability of such a "surgical strike" is overwhelming. With the United States' current nuclear triad—land-based ICBMs, submarine-launched ballistic missiles, and bombers—the possibility of all the missiles being hit before launch is not only remote but infinitesimal. To spread the word about a strategic disadvantage is therefore inaccurate and ir- responsible because it encourages a militaristic response and never- ending arms race spiral. Because the president claimed the Soviets had a definite advantage, most persons believed it.

The "window of vulnerability" argument is just one dangerous myth about nuclear weapons. The danger here is the attitude that the Soviets possess military supremacy. But a far more dangerous attitude begins with those who believe that victory in nuclear war is possible.

Former Secretary of Defense Caspar Weinberger held the view that the United States could win a nuclear war. In Weinberger's 1984–1988 defense guidance document he stated, "Should deterrence fail and strategic nuclear war with the U.S.S.R. occur, the United States must prevail and be able to force the Soviet Union to seek earliest termination of hostilities on terms favorable to the United States."[24] Joining Weinberger in this view are such "players" as Col- in S. Gray, State Department consultant and member of the Commit- tee on the Present Danger. Gray wrote, "No one can possibly design a nuclear strategy that entails anything less than somewhere between 5 and 20 million front-deaths . . . [but 20 million] is damage from which we can recover."[25] Gray called for the "demise of the Soviet state" in an article entitled "Victory Is Possible."[26]

Perhaps the most eery of the "winnable war" statements came from the lips of T. K. Jones, deputy undersecretary of defense for strategic and theater nuclear forces. Jones's views are "typical of those at the core of the Reagan administration," wrote Robert Scheer. "The only difference is that T.K. was more outspoken than the others." Jones quite seriously argued that nuclear war is win- nable. "Dig a hole, cover it with a couple of doors and then throw three feet of dirt on top—It's the dirt that does it—if there are enough shovels to go around, everybody's going to make it.''[27] Such views are rendered all the more morbid by the tone and stature of the people who hold them.

If enough believe that we can lead in the arms race or win a nuclear war, then defense budgets will follow suit. We will try to make the dream a reality. So $120 billion spent for defense in 1980 may leap to $344 in 1990.[28]

Still others believe that we can achieve a lead over our enemy. Significant ''advantages'' have been illusory for about twenty-five years. McNamara recalled that the United States possessed 5,000 strategic warheads in 1962. The Soviets had only 300. When the Cuban missile crisis occurred that year, some people in the White House recommended an attack on the Soviet Union. But McNamara knew that if the Soviets retaliated, tens of their missiles would reach U.S. territory, causing millions of deaths. He could not endorse the bombing because the loss of so many lives would be unacceptable to any responsible decision maker. If an advantage of seventeen to one in strategic warheads was not an ''acceptable advantage,'' can either side ever attain a huge lead again? It is doubtful.[29]

Related to the confrontational policy of pursuing an elusive advantage is the idea that if the Soviets don't like it, it must be good. This presumption has long been a part of the U.S.-Soviet relations, and it reared its head again after the Iceland summit. Before the Reykjavik meeting 62 percent of Americans polled approved of Star Wars. But after Americans discovered Gorbachev's opposition to the vision of an umbrella defense, this number jumped to 75 percent.[30] This is belligerence, not rationality; a use of heart, not of mind.

Two lessons can be drawn. The first is that leaders should not let important decisions about foreign policy be swayed by the mood swings of an uninformed electorate. Strategy decisions about nuclear weaponry are delicate and important, far too important to be left to the climate of popular opinion. A second lesson is that rationality and military needs must determine how we handle strategic matters. One-upmanship gives us the illusory feeling that we are ahead in a game, that if we press and compete just a little harder we can prevail. In the nuclear age, when both countries combined have 50,000 lethal warheads, ''prevailing'' loses its meaning. McNamara claimed that parity existed in 1962. If there were sound reasons for drawing that conclusion twenty-five years ago, then parity is here to stay. Moreover, parity is good. As long as a ''balance of terror'' exists, no country will risk an attack. Belligerence, then, is an excessive response to the U.S.-Soviet confrontation.

Since belligerence and defeatism as strategic attitudes are encouraged by the contradictory impulses of the U.S. public, decisions about how to handle the Soviets should be free of public pressure. Consider that Americans want their leaders to talk to the Soviets and reach agreements, but at the same time they hold a deep distrust of the Soviets' agreements. What to do? A *Washington Post* news poll revealed that voters favored arms reduction over SDI, until they were told that that their president thinks that SDI is more important than reductions.[31] With these kinds of fickle tendencies, the attitudes of the majority are probably not of any value.

What has value? What is a proper posture for the United States to take? A nonbelligerent attitude seems appropriate. If we come to the negotiating table, we must realize that negotiations are a means only, even if the U.S. public sees talking as an end. Talks with Soviet leaders are of value only if they are in the interest of both countries. In order to make prudent negotiations, we must have a philosophy of what is strategically prudent and what isn't.

This second point actually has primary importance, because we cannot deal without an overarching policy that specifies what good dealing is. For example, do we want to preserve a policy of mutually assured destruction, which justifies any level of arms buildup so long as it guarantees that we will destroy any attacker? Or do we want a policy of minimum assured deterrence—which says that the lowest level of warheads that still deters is best, because it is safe and cheap?

If we desire minimum assured deterrence, then we desire arms reductions. Consequently, as Senator Nunn urged, our preoccupation with Star Wars is "out of focus." It's out of focus because it blocks the goal of reducing Soviet offensive weapons, a goal that Reagan said he wants to achieve.

### 6.   STAR WARS?

Whether Star Wars should be heavily funded, researched, and deployed depends not only on its technical efficiency but on how it is perceived. The perceptions of the Reagan administration, NATO leaders, and the Soviet leadership vary, and then the scientific community has its own analysis, stripped of political bias.

To Reagan, Star Wars will be a guarantee of international security, a system that will repel enemy missiles the way "a roof repels rain."

Reagan has also distrusted deterrence, likening mutually assured destruction to two gunfighters aiming pistols, each daring the other to shoot first. Caspar Weinberger extended this view, urging that Star Wars will one day provide "security" and "stability" and "rid us of the specter of nuclear war."[32] By the beginning of 1988, over $12 billion has been voted for the SDI program since the president's March 1983 speech. But this confidence in the utility of Star Wars is countered by what many see as its damaging political and military implications.

The Kremlin holds a different attitude. Far from being a system that will further international security and provide a lasting peace, the Soviets perceive SDI as an aggressive defensive system that aims to achieve a first-strike capability against them. The Soviet general secretary's first tangle with Star Wars occurred at Reykjavik. After that summit he blamed the United States' hold on Star Wars for the failure to achieve any substantial agreements. Since then, he has claimed, "We can develop an anti-STAR WARS program,"[33] although he would prefer not to have this extra burden on the Soviet economy. As for President Reagan's statement that the United States would share the defensive shield with the Soviets, Gorbachev was incredulous, saying the United States would hold on to Star Wars for themselves. So assuming that the Soviets take the deployment of an effective space defensive system seriously, and since Reykjavik, there have been signs that they take it less seriously, they will react with a concentrated response. If they desire, they could increase their number of ICBMs to 30,000 by the year 2000 well in advance of any effective system.

Indeed, the perception of an effective shield would almost certainly step up the arms race and increase all sorts of measures by the Soviets to thwart its efficiency. For one, it will destroy the anti-ballistic missile (ABM) treaty, the most important arms control agreement to date. Second, it will inspire the growth of offensive and defensive systems on the Soviet side. Moreover, as long as Star Wars research and testing continues, it will impede the prospects for improvement in the tensions between the two superpowers.

Just four days after the president's speech on Star Wars, Yuri Andropov replied, "STAR WARS . . . is a bid to disarm the Soviet Union in the face of the U.S. nuclear threat."[34] If the tables were reversed, what would the U.S. response be? If probabilities decreed that the Soviets could deploy an effective defense against our long-range missiles, and perhaps other bombs, we would certainly make every effort to ensure that at least some of our missiles could penetrate. Why, then, should we expect a different perception and a less aggressive response from the Soviets?

How do the Europeans perceive Star Wars, and what implications might it have for the alliance? At first, Europeans feared that if SDI were effective, it would isolate the United States, returning it to its pre-1941 notion of fortress America. NATO countries as a result would be divorced or "decoupled" from the U.S. security blanket. Indeed, the United States would sit safely beneath its shield while the Europeans were all the more vulnerable to Soviet attack.

Europeans also wondered why a president who had tried so hard to give the United States a strategic advantage would turn around and cast off nearly four decades of a strategic policy that states that deterrence—the threat of one's offensive capability—is the way to play the game in the nuclear age. Without prior consultation Europe discovered that Washington, exceedingly confident with the prospect of exotic defenses, was ready to negotiate a zero option, eliminating NATO's sophisticated and powerful intermediate-range missiles, missiles that were so politically difficult to get in the first place. Some of these reservations went back to 1985. Near universal rejection of Reagan's SDI followed when it first became public. European strategists doubted its scientific feasibility and feared its destabilizing impact on the precarious Soviet–U.S. nuclear balance. It was also seen as a rejection of the long-standing Atlantic doctrine of nuclear deterrence, the foundation of NATO defense strategy. NATO partners are predicting that SDI research will only trigger a new escalation of the arms race. Citing their own interests, why would European governments, who believe that their weapons contributed to the peace in Europe for forty years, want to abandon deterrence for something they are unsure of. The pursuit of Star Wars funding and research is but another action of the Reagan administration causing consternation, uncertainty, and insecurity in the alliance.

Quite apart from the political and military ramifications of Star Wars deployment, a veritable plethora of scientific and technical criticisms cast doubt on its efficacy. The officer in charge of the program, Lieutenant James Abrahamson, admitted, "A perfect defense is not a realistic thing."[35] Defense Department Undersecretary Richard DeLauer made it plain in a conversation with Senator Sam Nunn of Georgia that he could not foresee any level of defense that would make our own offensive systems unnecessary.[36] If a space shield stopped 95 percent of incoming warheads, it still wouldn't save either society from disintegration. Said DeLauer, "There's no way an enemy can't overwhelm your defenses if he wants to badly enough."[37] Much of the literature criticizes the utility of particle beams and lasers in killing ICBMs. The anti–Star Wars technical record is vast.

What seems certain, aside from all the military countermeasures designed to destroy SDI, is that the deployment of Star Wars will stimulate the strongest possible Soviet response.

Why would anyone expect the Soviets to sit still while we disarm them with a protective shield? The Soviets will squirm if they believe the shield will one day be 100 percent effective. They will squirm in a world with or without missiles.

The net effect? At best, it will cause them to rearm; at worst, to launch a preemptive strike. When such negative consequences attach to the research and deployment of Star Wars and are added to the doubts that it will never be technically efficient, why deploy it? Why wrap the U.S. flag around it as if to say, A vote for Star Wars is a vote for America?

Whether STAR WARS is worthwhile has to do with military dynamics. It has nothing to do with visions, longings of the heart, or nationalistic fervor.

### 7.  NUCLEAR FRIGHT

In the many discussions about how to conduct NATO–Warsaw Pact foreign policy, emotionalism always has its day. But elements of nuclear fright must be eliminated if reasoned decisions about the weapons are to be made. A kind of controlled hysteria has always surrounded the nuclear debate.

C. P. Snow predicted in 1960 that World War III would occur inside of ten years.[38] Philosopher Paul Ramsey claimed that threatening nations to keep them from attacking is like attaching babies to bumpers of automobiles to force motorists to drive more carefully.[39] Jonathan Schell, nuclear fright artist par excellence, claimed that since there is a chance of nuclear catastrophe, we must treat that probability as if it were a certainty.[40] It is a moral imperative, according to this logic, to abolish nuclear arms.

If relations between nuclear-capable nations are best founded on a basis of security, then apocalyptic fears of nuclear annihilation cannot rule the roost. Fear cannot be a criterion for sound judgment. Reason is not opposed to morality. So many fears and dark predictions come forth about thermonuclear weapons. So many assurances of imminent doom are voiced. What of the wise man's saying, Where there is less fear, there is generally less danger?

Until an alternate deterrent can be found, the weapons are here to stay. They cannot be disinvented, as Margaret Thatcher said in defense of a nuclear England. Until a time arrives when they are obsolete, NATO had better base its security needs on the magnitude of the threat posed by the enemy. Little else is relevant—certainly not what fear leads us to.

## 8.   NUCLEAR DETERRENCE

One of the lessons of Star Wars is, No strategy ought to replace deterrence as a nuclear policy. To this point in time, no other alternative is in the field. A will avoid striking B if he knows that B will retaliate, causing unacceptable destruction to A. The gains that A could possibly achieve are thus balanced by the losses he would incur. In a world where there are few certainties, the strongest available probabilities must be set in motion.

A military posture that undercuts deterrence had better have a strong rationale. Up to this time, no strategist has conceived of a more effective military posture than one that threatens any attacker with the guarantee that he will be attacked. A balance of power provides no certainty that an opponent will not attack. But possessing a second-strike capability can threaten an opponent with unacceptable losses of lives and material. Allowing an opponent a second-strike capability also would lessen the insecurity the opponent would feel in a crisis. Strategic balance, not unilateral advantage, fuels stability. Stability decreases the threat of global war, which in turn allows people to direct their energies toward other matters.

The figures in Table 1 reveal that the forces of both superpowers are in rough parity. The present condition of balance is extremely appealing to a believer in deterrence.[41]

Table 1.
The Forces of the United States and the Soviet Union

|  | United States | | Soviet Union | |
|---|---|---|---|---|
|  | *Launchers* | *Warheads* | *Launchers* | *Warheads* |
| Land missiles | 1,010 | 2,110 | 1,398 | 6,420 |
| Submarine missiles | 640 | 6,656 | 944 | 3,216 |
| Bombers | 260 | 4,080 | 160 | 1,080 |
| Total | 1,910 | 12,846 | 2,502 | 10,716 |

One tenth of either side's forces could devastate the other side. Several conclusions follow from this. One, since the explosive power of either side's arsenal is more than necessary to meet defense needs, we have no need for further buildup.

Two, to maintain and upgrade existing forces, there must be testing. Testing is part of deterrence, so a nod for testing is a no to nuclear freezing. The slogan nuclear freeze has achieved an undeserved respect ever since the Democratic convention in 1984. Like many slogans, it has not been carefully considered. A freeze implies no testing of future weapons and no upgrading of existing arsenals. Although it is not necessary to continue to test new weapons, it is necessary to test what already exists.

Third, although arms control is a value, arms reduction may not be. For instance, if the United States were to reduce its ICBMs in exchange for a reduction in Soviet missiles in East Europe, this would be a bad exchange, since the United States is already far behind in its number of ICBMs and is always looking to reduce the Soviets' ICBM force.

Many of the attacks on the doctrine of nuclear deterrence, including those by the Catholic bishops and Jonathan Schell, point out that deterrence may fail. Thus, it is argued, deterrence must only be a temporary measure, as the bishops argue, or we will, as Churchill claimed, "return to the stone age on the gleaming wings of science."[42] But to attack our nuclear predicament is only a partial truth; it must be shown that a better alternative exists.

Leftist governments in Europe, like the West German Social Democratic party or the British Labour party, would, if given the chance, remove not only the U.S. Pershing IIs and cruises but all the remaining European missiles as well. Despite their good intentions, their philosophy of denuclearization would return us to the stone age more quickly than the present policy of deterrence. David Calleo pointed out that without nuclear weapons it's difficult to believe Europe would have avoided a war for the last forty-three years. Present European policy makers believe, for the most part, that nuclear deterrence is safer than conventional deterrence. The possibility of war with the threat of nuclear retaliation is far less likely than without that threat.

Jonathan Schell wrote eloquently for the abolition of atomic weapons. His points concerned nuclear winter, the gradual cooling of the earth due to particles keeping out the sun after an atomic explosion; the destruction of the ozone that would cause harmful ultraviolet rays to penetrate the atmosphere; the resulting changes in the world's weather patterns; and the short- and long-term effects of global fallout. "We gain security through the risk of extinction," pleaded Schell, "which is totally unsatisfactory to the peace movement." All this is frighteningly accurate; no one wants to witness the detonation of even a single megaton weapon. Nonetheless, the nightmare, described by Schell and often captured on films that reveal the rippling effects of heat blast and fallout, will come more as a result of abolition than deterrence.[43]

No doubt, world security rests on paradox—hence, the words of Churchill: "Safety will be the sturdy child of terror and survival the twin brother of annihilation."[44] These horrific weapons are useful nonetheless—useful to the extent that they'll never be used. Thus, the bishops' proposal that NATO should pledge never to be the first to use the weapons is absurd. The deterrent of the weapons comes, as Krauthammer insightfully argued, from not only the weapons themselves but the readiness to use them.[45]

Deterrence is not license for nuclear "redundance" or "overkill." Nor is it a demigod doctrine; rather, it is a means to the moral goal of human survival.

## 9.  THE INFLUENCE OF PROPAGANDA

If fear, an antidote to sound judgment, should be resisted, so should any propaganda that sways a nation from its firm convictions.

Leaders of NATO ought to decide its policies freely. This means steeling themselves against the views of such persons as Soviet Foreign Minister Eduard Shevardnaze, Gorbachev, and even Labour leader Neil Kinnock, who are campaigning to upset the status quo, to show their "commitment" to world peace. Often commitment is only posturing to bring advantages to themselves.

Any propaganda about the state of peace between nations like the Soviet Union and the United States must be looked at skeptically. The possibility of genuine peace that can exist between totalitarian countries and democratic ones has not been made clear. What can be expected between powers so different is not peace, but coexistence.

Instances of propaganda abound. In Vienna, soon after the Reykjavik summit, Shevardnaze accused the United States of a "mothballed set of views and approaches" to arms control, despite the fact that this was only a "mini-summit," with no major deals on the agenda.[46] He also blasted Europeans, especially the British and French, for wanting "to protect their alleged privileges as nuclear states." Western Europe, he concluded, "seemed to be backing off the chance to move toward a world free of nuclear weapons." He continued, "Are our missiles in Europe a threat, while theirs are just an assortment of chocolates in a fancy box?" This remark, as Sir Geoffrey Howe said, is just a travesty of the truth, if intended to include the British. Two reasons make this so:

1. The chance of a nuclear-free world is not one to back away from. It is one to run from. For taking such a chance, Europe might be scalded in no time.

2. Yes, the Soviet missiles are a threat; no, the European ones are not. The European missiles are defensive in nature. Since NATO was formed, they've been defensive. To suggest otherwise is to be guilty of verbal warfare, warfare that no one with a mind should listen to.

While the discussion of cuts at Reykjavik alarmed conservatives, it gave a shot in the arm to Europe's left. Europe can now look at the historic new decision and say, See, the superpowers want there to be no nuclear weapons in the world. With medicine like this, who needs poison?

Another bit of recurrent propaganda is a myth perpetrated by several U.S. administrations—the myth of Soviet military superiority. It is this myth, of course, that justifies continual buildups. Several recent administrations have used the fear that we are behind in the race in order to get greater defense outlays. However, the data in Table 1 show that no one nation leads the other by any measure worth talking about.

## 10. DÉTENTE, AGAIN?

Finally, a rebirth of détente should be avoided. To allow détente is to open a door for the Soviets, giving them a chance to practice the methods of conquest that they use to split the alliance, the methods discussed in Chapter 4. To set a policy that says relax tensions is to play into the Soviets' hands, not ours.

Persons in the past have said détente is vital, because without it we will have a nuclear holocaust. Again, this is a use of fear, not reason. It is a frightful either/or, nothing more. We should not attempt to conciliate the Soviet Union at all costs. Détente is a policy the Soviets use to silence criticisms against them: They can always maintain that any attack on them hurts the spirit of détente.

If the premises for détente are the need to control arms and to avoid war, then détente is important. However, negative détente allows the appearance of peace while providing a cover for all sorts of aggressions. As I have mentioned, the Soviets have exploited the appearance of détente in order to develop arms, step up ideological warfare, and insinuate their views into the NATO alliance. Clausewitz's famous expression was "War is the pursuit of diplomacy by other means."[47] The Soviets in the past have used détente for the same purpose.

Many people have believed that if we cooperate with Moscow in enough ways, an atmosphere of good will will take over. Our rivalry with the Soviet Union will cease. Détente leads us to embrace expectations that are illusory.

Détente leads nations to let down their guards, even to the point of trading national security-related technology. Europe seems to need a reminder on this point: They have let down their guard and are extremely compliant with Soviet demands.

U.S. policy makers must first understand the psychological drama that is occurring. Only then can effective measures be taken to counter Europe's drift and reestablish the alliance so that the West can face the future strongly united.

# *Notes*

## INTRODUCTION

1. *New York Times*, April 7, 1985, 25.
2. *Wall Street Journal*, June 8, 1986, 8.
3. John Palmer, *Europe Without America?* (New York: Oxford University Press, 1987), 4.
4. Daniel Lang, "A Reporter At Large: The Bank Drama," *The New Yorker*, November 25, 1974, 56–126.
5. Palmer, *Europe*, 4.
6. Robert Jay Lifton, *The Future of Immortality* (New York: Basic Books, 1982), 201.
7. Lang, "Drama," 114.
8. *Wall Street Journal*, June 8, 1986, 8.
9. Thomas H. Naylor, *The Gorbachev Strategy* (Lexington, Mass.: Lexington Books, 1988), 36.
10. Strobe Talbot, *The Russians and Reagan* (New York: Vintage Books, 1984), 63.
11. See Andrei Gromyko, "The International Situation," *Vital Speeches*, July 15, 1983, p. 675.
12. Naylor, *Strategy*, 35.
13. Jeffrey Record and David B. Rivkin, Jr., "Defending Post-INF Europe," *Foreign Affairs* (Spring 1988): Vol. 66, No. 4, 753.
14. Richard Pipes, "How to Cope with the Soviet Threat: A Long-Term Strategy for the West," *Commentary*, August 1984, 16.
15. Both articles in *Guardian*, June 14, 1986, 13–4.
16. Tim Wells, *444 Days: The Hostages Remember* (New York: Harcourt, Brace, Jovanovich, 1984), 444.
17. Christopher Lasch, *The Minimal Self* (New York: W.W. Norton, 1984), 112.
18. Lasch, *Minimal Self*, 89.
19. Elizabeth Kubler-Ross, *On Death and Dying* (New York: Macmillan, 1969), 107.

20. Robert S. McNamara, *Blundering Into Disaster* (New York: Pantheon Books, 1986), 119.

21. Zhores A. Medvedev, *Gorbachev* (New York: W.W. Norton, 1986), 213.

22. Naylor, *Strategy*, 38.

23. Medvedev, *Gorbachev*, 216.

24. Thomas Butson, *Gorbachev: A Biography* (New York: Stein and Day, 1986), 211.

25. *Economist*, April 14, 1986. "Kinnock is Labor Hopeful."

26. Harry Gelman, *The Brezhnev Politburo and the Decline of Detente* (Ithaca, N.Y.: Cornell Univ. Press, 1984).

27. Albert Memmi, *Dependence* (Boston: Beacon Press, 1984), 16.

28. Richard Brockman. "Notes While Being Hijacked," *Atlantic*, December 1976, 75.

## CHAPTER 2

1. Daniel Lang, "A Reporter At Large: The Bank Drama," *The New Yorker*, November 25, 1974, 56.

2. Sympathy for the aggressor is one of the essential characteristics of what is now labeled Stockholm Syndrome.

3. Lang, "Drama," 121.

4. Lang, "Drama," 59.

5. Lang, "Drama," 117.

6. Lang, "Drama," 122.

7. Patricia Hearst, *Every Secret Thing* (Garden City, New York: Doubleday, 1982), 312.

8. Hearst, *Secret Thing*, 286.

9. Hearst, *Secret Thing*, 114.

10. Hearst, *Secret Thing*, 181.

11. Brian M. Jenkins, "Hostages and Their Captors—Friends and Lovers," *The Rand Corporation*, October 1975, 11.

12. Jenkins, "Hostages," p. 9.

13. Sir Geoffrey Jackson, *Surviving the Long Night* (New York: Vanguard Press, 1974).

14. "Terrorism," *State Department Bulletin*, December 1985, 77.

15. "Terrorism," *State Department Bulletin*, December 1985, 79.

16. "The 38 Hours: Trial by Terror," *Time*, March 21, 1977. p. 37.

17. "The 38 Hours: Trial by Terror," p. 39.

18. "The 38 Hours: Trial by Terror," p. 42.

19. "The 38 Hours: Trial by Terror," p. 43.

20. Richard Brockman, "Notes While Being Hijacked," *Atlantic*, December 1976, 72.

21. What follows in this chapter is a psychological analysis of hostages, Stockholm Syndrome, and captivity.

22. Kurt Carlson, *One American Must Die* (New York: Cangdon and Weed, 1986), 74.

23. Sylvia Jacobsen, "Individual and Group Response to Confinement in a Skyjacked Plane," *American Journal of Orthopsychiatry* (April 1973), 460.

24. Carlson, *One American*, 67.

25. *New York Times*, September 6, 1986. "Palestinians Sieze Pan Am Jet," p. 1.

26. "Palestinians Sieze Pan Am Jet," p. 1.

27. "Palestinians Sieze Pan Am Jet," p. 12.

28. ABC News, *Nightline*, July 30, 1985, show no. 1095.

29. ABC News, *Nightline*, July 2, 1985, show no. 1072.

30. ABC News, *Nightline*, July 2, 1985, show no. 1072.

31. Robert Jay Lifton, *Thought Reform and the Psychology of Totalism* (New York: W.W. Norton, 1969), 71.

32. Sigmund Freud, *Inhibitions, Symptoms and Anxiety* (New York: W.W. Norton, 1959), 6.

33. Robert G. Hillman, "The Psychopathology of Being Held Hostage," *American Journal of Psychiatry* (September 1981): 1193-97.

34. Lang, "Drama," 112.

35. Carlson, *One American*, 91.

36. Moorhead Kennedy, *The Ayatollah in the Cathedral* (New York: Hill and Wang, 1986), 111.

37. Barcuh Spinoza, "The Ethics" in *The Rationalists* (New York: Anchor Books, 1974), 179-405.

38. See Terrence Des Pres, *The Survivor: An Anatomy of Life in the Death Camps* (New York: Washington Square Press, 1976); Bruno Bettelheim, *The Informed Heart* (New York: The Free Press, 1960).

39. Viktor E. Frankl, *Man's Search for Meaning* (New York: Washington Square Press, 1984), 64.

40. Jacobson, "Skyjacked Plane," 462.

41. Anna Freud, *The Ego and the Mechanisms of Defense* (New York: International Universities Press, 1937).

42. See Joe E. Dimsdale, "The Coping Behaviors of Nazi Concentration Camp Survivors," *American Journal of Psychiatry* (July 1974):792-97. Vol 131, no. 7.

43. Dimsdale, "Coping Behaviors," 792.

44. Tim Wells, *444 Days: The Hostages Remember* (New York: Harcourt, Brace, Jovanovich, 1984).

45. Douglas Valentine, *The Hotel Tacloban* (New York: Avon Books, 1984), 142.

46. For a fine discussion of the problem of evil, see Ed L. Miller, *An Invitation to Philosophy* (New York: McGraw Hill, 1987).

47. Dimsdale, "Coping Behaviors," 794.

48. Wells, *444 Days*, 167.

49. Wells, *444 Days*, 146.

50. Bruno Bettelheim, *Surviving and Other Essays* (New York: Vintage Books, 1980), 63.

51. Bettelheim, *Surviving*, 65.

52. Zalin Grant, *Survivors: American POWs in Vietnam* (New York: Berkeley Books, 1985), 108.

53. Patricia Hearst, *Every Secret Thing* (Garden City, N.Y.: Doubleday, 1982), 280.

54. Leo Tolstoy, *The Cossacks and Other Stories* (New York: Penguin, 1982), 99.

55. Dimsdale, "Coping Behaviors," 796.

56. Hearst, *Secret Thing*, 246.

57. Russell Noyes, "Depersonalization in the Face of Life Threatening Dangers: A Description." *Psychiatry* Vol. 31 (February 1976): 157–172.

58. Sigmund Freud, "The Splitting of the Ego in Self-Defense" in *The Complete Psychological Works of Sigmund Freud* (London: Hogarth Press, 1955) vol. 2, pp. 118–126.

59. Jacob Ecclestone, "Stress: Making Friends of Enemies" in *International Journal of Offender Therapy and Comparitive Criminology* Vol. 3 (November 1980): 185–207.

60. Bettelheim, *Surviving*, 102.

61. Carlson, *One American*, 108.

62. Bettelheim, *Surviving*, 47.

63. Hannah Arendt, *The Origins of Totalitarianism* (New York: Harcourt, Brace, Jovanovich, 1979), 161.

64. Frank A. Bolz, Jr., *How to Be a Hostage and Live* (Secaucus, N.J.: Lyle Stewart, 1987), 41.

65. Bolz, *How to be a Hostage*, 63.

66. Robert Jay Lifton, *The Future of Immortality* (New York: Basic Books, 1982), 187.

67. Bettelheim, *Surviving*, 71.

68. Lifton, *Immortality*, 18.

69. Brockman, "Notes," 79.

70. Brockman, "Notes," 80.

71. Valentine, *Tacloban*, 61.

72. Wells, *444 Days*, 136.

73. Wells, *444 Days*, 207.

74. Thomas A. Sancton, "Smoothing the Way," *Time*, November 17, 1980, 41.

75. *New Republic*, "Soviet Ethnos," July 14, 1986, 19.

## CHAPTER 3

1. David Shapiro, *Autonomy and Rigid Character* (New York: Basic Books, 1981), 41.

2. Bruno Bettelheim, *Surviving and Other Essays* (New York: Vintage Books, 1980), 29.

3. Albert Memmi, *Dependence* (Boston: Beacon Press, 1984), 26.

4. Robert Jay Lifton, *The Future of Immortality* (New York: Basic Books, 1982), 218.

5. Bettelheim, *Surviving*, 36.

6. Brian M. Jenkins, "Hostages and Their Captors—Friends and Lovers," *The Rand Corporation*, October 1975, 11.

7. Sigmund Freud, *Complete Works*, Vol. 3 (New York: International Universities Press, 1937), 160.

8. Anna Freud, *The Ego and Mechanisms of Defense* (New York: International Universities Press, 1937), 112.

9. Anna Freud, *Mechanisms of Defense*, 116.

10. Anna Freud, *Mechanisms of Defense*, 119.

11. Bettelheim, *Surviving*, 49.

12. Jean Piaget, *Six Psychological Studies* (New York: Vintage Books, 1968).

13. Piaget, *Psychological Studies*, 49.

14. Anna Freud, *Mechanisms of Defense*, 106.

## CHAPTER 4

1. Richard J. Barnet, *The Alliance* (New York: Simon & Schuster, 1983), 49.
2. Barnet, *Alliance*, 72.
3. Barnet, *Alliance*, 78.
4. Barnet, *Alliance*, 87.
5. Barnet, *Alliance*, 114.
6. Barnet, *Alliance*, 118.
7. Barnet, *Alliance*, 109.
8. Barnet, *Alliance*, 114.
9. Barnet, *Alliance*, 124.
10. Barnet, *Alliance*, 174.
11. Barnet, *Alliance*, 247.
12. Barnet, *Alliance*, 282.
13. Barnet, *Alliance*, 350.
14. Jonathan Schell, *The Fate of the Earth* (New York: Alfred A. Knopf, 1982).
15. Schell has elsewhere pointed out that the difference in destruction depends upon electromagnetic pulse (blast) and heat, both of which are a function of the distance of objects from the point of explosion. See "The Effects of Nuclear Bombs" in *Moral Problems* (New York: West Publishing Company, 1988), 382–387.
16. Schell, *Fate*, 146.
17. Joseph S. Nye, Jr., *Nuclear Ethics* (New York: Macmillan, 1986), 18.
18. Richard Pipes, *Survival Is Not Enough: Soviet Realities and America's Future* (New York: Simon & Schuster, 1984), 31.
19. Thomas Powers, *Thinking About the Next War* (New York: New American Library, 1976).
20. NATO Generals, *Generals for Peace and Disarmament* (New York: Universe Books, 1984).
21. George F. Kennan, *The Nuclear Delusion* (New York: Pantheon Books, 1976).
22. Gwyn Prins, ed., *The Nuclear Crisis Reader* (New York: Vintage Books, 1984).
23. NATO Generals, *Peace and Disarmament*, 118.
24. NATO Generals, *Peace and Disarmament*, 26.
25. John Arthur, ed., *Morality and Moral Controversies* (Englewood Cliffs, N.J.: Prentice-Hall, 1986), 288.
26. Pipes, *Survival*, 114.
27. NATO Generals, *Peace and Disarmament*, 101.
28. NATO Generals, *Peace and Disarmament*, 93.
29. NATO Generals, *Peace and Disarmament*, 93.
30. Melvyn Krauss, *How NATO Weakens the West* (New York: Simon & Schuster, 1986), 107.
31. Kennan, *Delusion*, 14.
32. Kennan, *Delusion*, 27.
33. Kennan, *Delusion*, 42.
34. Kennan, *Delusion*, 44.
35. Douglas Lackey "Missiles and Morals: A Utilitarian Look at Nuclear Deterrence" in *Morality and Moral Controversies*, ed. Arthur. (New Jersey: Prentice Hall, 1981) 250–59.
36. Prins, ed., *Crisis Reader*, 72.

37. Prins, ed., *Crisis Reader*, 73.

38. Prins, ed., *Crisis Reader*, 86.

39. Prins, ed., *Crisis Reader*, 161.

40. Pipes, *Survival*, 148.

41. Pipes, *Survival*, 157.

42. Pipes, *Survival*, 168.

43. Pipes, *Survival*, 198.

44. Helmut Schmidt, *A Grand Strategy for the West* (New Haven: Yale University Press, 1985), 111.

45. Pipes, *Survival*, 108.

46. Timothy Stanley, *NATO in Transition* (New York: Macmillan, 1965), 111.

## CHAPTER 5

1. Roy Medvedev, *Krushchev* (Garden City, N.Y.: Macmillan, 1983).

2. Medvedev, *Krushchev*, 116.

3. Benjamin Netanvahu, *Terrorism: How the West Can Win* (New York: Farrar, Straus, Giroux, 1986).

4. Henry A. Kissinger, *Nuclear Weapons and Foreign Policy* (New York: W.W. Norton, 1957), 112.

5. Henry A. Kissinger, *The Troubled Partnership: A Reappraisal of the Atlantic Alliance* (New York: McGraw Hill, 1965), 49.

6. Theodore Draper, *Present History: On Nuclear War, Detente, and Other Controversies* (New York: Vintage Books, 1973), 212.

7. Draper, *Present History*, 247.

8. Gwyn Prins, ed., *The Nuclear Crisis Reader* (New York: Vintage Books, 1984), 162.

9. Medvedev, *Gorbachev*, 140.

10. Richard F. Starr, *U.S.S.R. Foreign Policies After Detente* (Stanford, Calif.: Hoover Press, 1985), 111.

11. Richard Pipes, *Survival Is Not Enough: Soviet Realities and America's Future* (New York: Simon & Schuster), 212.

12. Starr, *After Detente*, 124.

13. Pipes, *Survival*, 72.

14. Pipes, *Survival*, 114.

15. Pipes, *Survival*, 121.

16. Pipes, *Survival*, 204.

17. Pipes, *Survival*, 211.

18. Pipes, *Survival*, 177.

19. Draper, *Present History*, 201.

20. Draper, *Present History*, 179.

21. Pipes, *Survival*, 248.

22. Pipes, *Survival*, 185.

23. Draper, *Present History*, 222.

24. Draper, *Present History*, 215.

25. Draper, *Present History*, 217.

26. Draper, *Present History*, 215.

27. Pipes, *Survival*, 208.

28. Draper, *Present History*, 216.
29. Arch Puddington, "The New Soviet Apologists," *Commentary*, November 1983, 36.
30. Draper, *Present History*, 218.
31. Draper, *Present History*, 222.
32. Draper, *Present History*, 219.
33. Pipes, *Survival*, 218.
34. Pipes, *Survival*, 235.
35. *World Press Review*, "Opinions on Salt II," July 1986.
36. *World Press Review*, "Opinions on Salt II," July 1986.
37. "The Sentry at the Gate: A Survey of NATO's Central Front," *The Economist*, August 30, 1986.
38. Pipes, *Survival*, 248.
39. Zbigniew Brzezinski, *Game Plan: How to Conduct the U.S.-Soviet Contest* (Boston: The Atlantic Monthly Press, 1986), 186.
40. Brzezinski, *Game Plan*, 207.
41. Brzezinski, *Game Plan*, 209.
42. Brzezinski, *Game Plan*, 201.

## CHAPTER 6

1. Harry Gelman, *The Brezhnev Politburo and the Decline of Detente* (Ithaca, N.Y.: Cornell Univ. Press, 1984), 212.
2. Milovan Djilas, *The New Class* (New York: Praeger, 1957).
3. Theodore Draper, *Present History: On Nuclear War, Detente, and Other Controversies* (New York: Vintage Books, 1973), 216.
4. Draper, *Present History*, 226.
5. Draper, *Present History*, 228.
6. Richard Pipes, *Survival Is Not Enough: Soviet Realities and America's Future* (New York: Simon & Schuster, 1984), 198.
7. Pipes, *Survival*, 209.
8. Draper, *Present History*, 212.
9. Strobe Talbott, *The Russians and Reagan* (New York: Vintage Books, 1984), 76.
10. Melvyn Krauss, *How NATO Weakens the West* (New York: Simon & Schuster, 1986), 105.
11. Krauss, *NATO*, 176.
12. Timothy Stanley, *NATO in Transition* (New York: MacMillan, 1965), 11.
13. Stanley, *NATO in Transition*, 83.

## CHAPTER 7

1. Seweryn Bialer, *The Soviet Paradox* (New York: Alfred A. Knopf, 1986), 276.
2. Marshall D. Shulman, "The Superpowers: Dance of the Dinosaurs," *Foreign Affairs* (Winter 1987-1988): Vol. 66, no. 3, 497.
3. Stephen Cohen, *Sovieticus* (New York: W.W. Norton, 1986), 91.
4. Cohen, *Sovieticus*, 94.
5. Cohen, *Sovieticus*, 71.

6. Richard M. Nixon, "Dealing with Gorbachev," *New York Times Magazine*, March 3, 1988, 27.

7. Thomas H. Naylor, *The Gorbachev Strategy* (Lexington, Mass.: Lexington Books), 142.

8. *Manchester Guardian Weekly*, "Gorbachev's Outlook," December 20, 1987, 8.

9. *Manchester Guardian Weekly*, "Gorbachev's Outlook," December 20, 1987, 8.

10. Shulman, "Dinosaurs," 497.

11. Cohen, *Sovieticus*, 148.

12. Mikhail Gorbachev, *New Thinking for Our Country and the World* (New York: Richardson and Steinman, 1987), 21.

13. Nixon, "Dealing with Gorbachev," 28.

14. Naylor, *Strategy*, 38.

15. Naylor, *Strategy*, 38.

16. Milan Svec, "Removing Gorbachev's Edge," *Foreign Policy* (Winter 1987–1988):148–65. Vol. 66, No. 2.

17. Philip Gold, "Pact and Impact: A Waiting Game," *Insight*, February 22, 1988, 15.

18. Gold, "Pact and Impact," 13.

19. Gold, "Pact and Impact," 15.

20. Gold, "Pact and Impact," 15.

21. Nixon, "Dealing with Gorbachev," 29.

22. Nixon, "Dealing with Gorbachev," 29.

23. Nixon, "Dealing with Gorbachev," 29.

24. Charles Krauthammer, "The Week Washington Lost Its Head," *New Republic*, January 4, 1988, 18.

25. Mikhail Gorbachev, *Perestroika* (New York: Harper & Row, 1987), 194.

26. Gorbachev, *Perestroika*, 207.

27. Gorbachev, *Perestroika*, 243.

28. Gorbachev, *Perestroika*, 191.

29. Gorbachev, *Perestroika*, 192.

30. Cohen, *Sovieticus*, 148.

31. Michio Kaku and Daniel Axelrod, *To Win A Nuclear War* (Boston: South End Press, 1987), 209.

32. John Palmer, *Europe Without America?* (New York: Oxford University Press, 1987), 55.

33. Palmer, *Europe*, 162.

34. A.M. Rosenthal, "Gorbachev's Hidden Agenda," *New York Times*, December 12, 1987, 24.

35. Krauthammer, "Lost Its Head," 18.

## CHAPTER 8

1. See especially Melvyn Krauss, *How NATO Weakens the West* (New York: Simon & Schuster, 1986).

2. Krauss, *NATO*, 107.

3. See "The Sentry at the Gate: A Survey of NATO's Central Front," *The Economist*, August 30, 1986.

4. Krauss, *NATO*, 186.

5. Krauss, *NATO*, 46.

6. Theodore Draper, *Present History: On Nuclear War, Detente, and Other Controversies* (New York: Vintage Books, 1973), 221.

7. Krauss, *NATO*, 53.

8. Krauss, *NATO*, 86.

9. Krauss, *NATO*, 114.

10. Krauss, *NATO*, 187.

11. Krauss, *NATO*, 236.

12. David P. Calleo, *Beyond American Hegemony* (New York: Basic books, 1987).

13. John Palmer, *Europe Without America?* (New York: Oxford University Press), 57.

14. Palmer, *Europe*, 57.

15. Philip M. Boffey, William J. Broad, Leslie H. Gelb, Charles Mohr, and Holcomb B. Noble, *Claiming the Heavens* (New York: Times Books, 1988), 144.

16. Palmer, *Europe*, 12.

17. See especially Jonathan Schell, *The Fate of the Earth* (New York: Alfred A. Knopf, 1982).

18. Thomas H. Naylor, *The Gorbachev Strategy* (Lexington, Mass.: Lexington Books), 38.

19. Naylor, *Strategy*, 38.

20. Robert S. McNamara, *Blundering Into Disaster* (New York: Pantheon Books, 1986), 42.

21. McNamara, *Disaster*, 47.

22. McNamara, *Disaster*, 46.

23. Robert Scheer, *With Enough Shovels* (New York: Vintage Books, 1983), 79.

24. McNamara, *Disaster*, 37.

25. Michio Kaku and Daniel Axelrod, *To Win a Nuclear War* (Boston: South End Press, 1987), 76.

26. Colin Gray, "Victory is Possible", *Foreign Policy*, Summer 1980.

27. Kaku and Axelrod, *Nuclear War*, 76.

28. Kaku and Axelrod, *Nuclear War*, 76.

29. Palmer, *Europe*, 72.

30. Andrew Kohut, "What Americans Want," *Foreign Policy* (Spring 1988):150-65. No. 7.

31. Kohut. "What Americans Want," 156.

32. Caspar W. Weinberger, "Arms Reduction and Deterrence," *Foreign Affairs* (Spring 1988):701. Vol. 66, No. 4.

33. Naylor, *Strategy*, 36.

34. Strobe Talbott and Michael Mandelbaum, *Reagan and Gorbachev* (New York: Vintage Books, 1987), 136.

35. William G. Hyland, ed. *The Reagan Foreign Policy* (New York: Meridian, 1987), 167.

36. Hyland, ed., *The Reagan Policy*, 167.

37. Hyland, ed., *The Reagan Policy*, 167.

38. Joseph S. Nye, Jr., *Nuclear Ethics* (New York: Macmillan, 1986), 33.

39. John Arthur, ed., *Morality and Moral Controversies* (Englewood Cliffs, N.J.: Prentice-Hall, 1986), 289.

40. Jonathan Schell, *The Fate of the Earth* (New York: Alfred A. Knopf, 1982), 135.

41. McNamara, *Disaster*, 41. These 1986 figures don't include weapons in Europe.

42. McNamara, *Disaster*, 87.

43. Schell, *Fate of the Earth*, 135.

44. Charles Krauthammer, "On Nuclear Morality," in *Morality and Moral Controversies*, ed. Arthur, 281.

45. Krauthammer, "Nuclear Morality," 280.

46. Mikhail Gorbachev, *Toward a Better World* (New York: Richardson and Steinman, 1987), 16.

47. Draper, *Present History*, 167.

# Selected Bibliography

## BOOKS

Arthur, John, ed. *Morality and Moral Controversies*. Englewood Cliffs, N.J.: Prentice-Hall, 1986.

Barnet, Richard J. *The Alliance*. New York: Simon & Schuster, 1983.

Bee, Helen. *The Developing Child*. New York: Harper & Row, 1985.

Bettelheim, Bruno. *The Informed Heart*. New York: The Free Press, 1960.

_____ . *Surviving and Other Essays*. New York: Vintage Books, 1980.

Bialer, Seweryn. *The Soviet Paradox*. New York: Alfred A. Knopf, 1986.

Boffey, Philip M.; Broad, William J.; Gelb, Leslie H.; Mohr, Charles; and Noble, Holcomb B. *Claiming the Heavens*. New York: Times Books, 1988.

Bolz, Frank A., Jr. *How to Be a Hostage and Live*. Secaucus, N.J.: Lyle Stuart, 1987.

Bottome, John. *The Balance of Terror: Nuclear Weapons and the Illusion of Security, 1945–1985*. Boston: Beacon Press, 1986.

Brzezinski, Zbigniew. *Game Plan: How to Conduct the U.S.–Soviet Contest*. Boston: The Atlantic Monthly Press, 1986.

Butson, Thomas. *Gorbachev: A Biography*. New York: Stein and Day, 1986.

Caldicott, Helen. *Missile Envy: The Arms Race and Nuclear War*. New York: Bantam Books, 1984.

Calleo, David P. *Beyond American Hegemony*. New York: Basic Books, 1987.

Carlson Kurt. *One American Must Die*. New York: Cangdon and Weed, 1986.

Charles, Daniel. *Nuclear Planning in NATO*. Cambridge: Ballinger, 1987.

Clarfield, Gerard H., and Wiecek, William M. *Nuclear America*. New York: Harper & Row, 1984.

Cohen, Stephen F. *The Rethinking the Soviet Experience*. Oxford: Oxford University Press, 1985.

_____ . *Sovieticus*. New York: W.W. Norton, 1986.

Des Pres, Terrence. *The Survivor: An Anatomy of Life in the Death Camps*. New York: Washington Square Press, 1976.

DiLeo, Joseph R. *Child Development, Analysis and Synthesis.* New York: Brunner/Mazel, 1977.

Draper, Theodore. *Present History: On Nuclear War, Detente, and Other Controversies.* New York: Vintage Books, 1973.

Durkheim, Emile. *Moral Education: A Study in the Theory of the Sociology of Education.* New York: Free Press, 1961.

Frankl, Viktor E. *Man's Search for Meaning.* New York: Washington Square Press, 1984.

Frankland, Mark. *The Sixth Continent: Mikhail Gorbachev and the Soviet Union.* New York: Harper & Row, 1987.

Freud, Anna. *The Ego and the Mechanisms of Defense.* New York: International Universities Press, 1937.

Freud, Sigmund. *Inhibitions, Symptoms and Anxiety.* New York: W. W. Norton, 1959.

———. *New Introductory Lectures on Psychoanalysis.* New York: W. W. Norton, 1965.

Gardner, Howard. *Developmental Psychology, An Introduction.* Boston and Toronto: Mentor Books, 1965.

Gervasi, Tom. *The Myth of Soviet Military Supremacy.* New York: Harper & Row, 1986.

Ginsburg, Herbert, and Opper, Sylvia. *Piaget's Theory of Intellectual Development.* Englewood Cliffs, N.J.: Prentice Hall, 1979.

Golman, Daniel, and Heller, David, eds. *The Pleasures of Psychology.* New York: American Library, 1986.

Gorbachev, Mikhail. *Perestroika.* New York: Harper & Row, 1987.

———. *Toward a Better World.* New York: Richardson and Steinman, 1987.

Goren, Roberta. *The Soviet Union and Terrorism.* London: George Allen & Unwin, 1984.

Grant, Zalin. *Survivors: American POWs in Vietnam.* New York: Berkeley Books, 1985.

Grinspoon, Lester. *The Long Darkness: Psychological and Moral Perspectives on Nuclear Winter.* New Haven: Yale University Press, 1986.

Hall, Calvin S., and Nordby, Vernon J. *A Primer of Jungian Psychology.* New York: New American Library, 1973.

Halliday, Fred. *The Making of the Second Cold War.* London: Verso, 1983.

Halprin, Morton H. *Nuclear Fallacy.* Cambridge: Ballinger, 1987.

Hearst, Patricia. *Every Secret Thing.* Garden City, N.Y.: Doubleday, 1982.

Hersey, John. *Hiroshima.* New York: Bantam Books, 1946.

Hollburg, David. *The Soviet Union and the Arms Race.* New Haven: Yale University Press, 1986.

Horelick, Arnold L., ed. *U.S.–Soviet Relations: The Next Phase.* Ithaca, N.Y.: Cornell University Press, 1986.

Horney, Karen. *Neurosis and Human Growth.* New York: W.W. Norton, 1950.

Hough, Jerry. *Russia and the West.* New York: Simon & Schuster, 1988.

Hyland, William G., ed. *The Reagan Foreign Policy.* New York: Meridian, 1987.

Johnson, Paul. *Modern Times: The World From the Twenties to the Eighties.* New York: Harper & Row, 1983.

Johnson, R. W. *Shootdown: Flight 007 and the American Connection.* New York: Viking, 1986.

Kaku, Michio, and Axelrod, Daniel. *To Win A Nuclear War.* Boston: South End Press, 1987.

Kennan, George F. *The Nuclear Delusion.* New York: Pantheon Books, 1976.

Kennedy, Moorhead. *The Ayatollah in the Cathedral.* New York: Hill and Wang, 1986.

Kennedy, Paul. *The Rise and Fall of the Great Powers.* New York: Random House, 1987.

Kissinger, Henry A. *Nuclear Weapons and Foreign Policy.* New York: W. W. Norton, 1957.

_____. *The Troubled Partnership: A Reappraisal of the Atlantic Alliance.* New York: McGraw Hill, 1965.

Kniazhinsky, Vsevold. *West European Integration: Its Policies and International Relations.* Moscow: Progress Publishers, 1984.

Kohlberg, Lawrence. *The Psychology of Moral Development, vols. 1 and 2.* San Francisco: Harper & Row, 1984.

Krauss, Melvyn. *How NATO Weakens the West.* New York: Simon & Schuster, 1986.

Kubler-Ross, Elizabeth. *On Death and Dying.* New York: Macmillan, 1969.

Laing, R. D. *The Divided Self.* New York: Penguin Books, 1986.

Lasch, Christopher. *The Minimal Self.* New York: W. W. Norton, 1984.

Lewin, Moshe. *The Gorbachev Phenomenon.* Los Angeles: University of California Press, 1988.

Lifton, Robert Jay. *Thought Reform and the Psychology of Totalism.* New York: W. W. Norton, 1969.

_____. *The Future of Immortality.* New York: Basic Books, 1982.

Luttwak, Edward N. *The Grand Strategy of the Soviet Union.* New York: St. Martin's Press, 1983.

May, Rollo. *The Meaning of Anxiety.* New York: Washington Square Press, 1950.

McNamara, Robert S. *Blundering into Disaster.* New York: Pantheon Books, 1986.

Medvedev, Zhores A. *Gorbachev.* New York: W. W. Norton, 1986.

Memmi, Albert. *Dependence.* Boston: Beacon Press, 1984.

Morris, Charles R. *Iron Destinies, Lost Opportunities.* New York: Harper & Row, 1988.

Naylor, Thomas H. *The Gorbachev Strategy.* Lexington, Mass.: Lexington Books, 1988.

NATO Generals. *Generals for Peace and Disarmament.* New York: Universe Books, 1984.

Netanyahu, Benjamin. *Terrorism: How the West Can Win.* New York: Farrar, Straus, Giroux, 1986.

Nliszi, Dr. Milos. *Auschwitz.* New York: Fawcett Crest, 1960.

Nomberg, Przytyk, Sara. *Auschwitz.* Chapel Hill: University of North Carolina Press, 1985.

Nye, Joseph S., Jr. *Nuclear Ethics.* New York: Macmillan, 1986.

_____; Graham, Allison T.; and Carnesale, Albert, eds. *Fateful Visions.* Cambridge: Ballinger, 1988.

Palmer, John. *Europe Without America?.* New York: Oxford University Press, 1987.

Piaget, Jean. *Six Psychological Studies.* New York: Vintage Books, 1968.

Pipes, Richard. *U.S.–Soviet Relations in the Era of Detente.* Boulder, Colo.: Westview Press, 1981.

_____. *Survival Is Not Enough: Soviet Realities and America's Future.* New York: Simon & Schuster, 1984.

Powaski, Ronald E. *March to Armageddon.* New York: Oxford University Press, 1987.

Powers, Thomas. *Thinking About the Next War.* New York: New American Library, 1976.

Prins, Gwyn, ed. *The Nuclear Crisis Reader.* New York: Vintage Books, 1984.

Rhodes, Richard. *The Making of the Atomic Bomb.* New York: Simon & Schuster, 1986.

Rieff, Philip. *Freud: The Mind of the Moralist.* Chicago: University of Chicago Press, 1979.

Santoli, Al. *Everything We Had: An Oral History of the Vietnam War by Thirty-Three American Soldiers Who Fought It.* New York: Ballantine Books, 1981.

Scheer, Robert. *With Enough Shovels.* New York: Vintage Books, 1983.

Schell, Jonathan. *The Fate of the Earth.* New York: Alfred A. Knopf, 1982.

————. *The Abolition.* New York: Avon Books, 1984.

Schmidt, Helmudt. *A Grand Strategy for the West.* New Haven: Yale University Press, 1985.

Schreiber, Flora Rheta. *Sybil.* New York: Warner Books, 1973.

Sejna, Jan. *We Will Bury You.* London: Sidgwick & Jackson, 1982.

Semler, Eric; Benjamin, James; and Gross, Adam. *The Language of Nuclear War.* New York: Harper & Row, 1987.

Shapiro, David. *Autonomy and Rigid Character.* New York: Basic Books, 1981.

Smith, Hedrick. *The Russians.* New York: Ballantine Books, 1976.

Spanier, John. *American Foreign Policy Since World War II.* New York: Praeger Publishers, 1977.

Spector, Leonard S. *The New Nuclear Nations.* New York: Vintage Books, 1985.

Starr, Richard F. *USSR Foreign Policies After Detente.* Stanford: Hoover Press, 1985.

Talbott, Strobe. *Deadly Gambits.* New York: Vintage Books, 1984.

————. *The Russians and Reagan.* New York: Vintage Books, 1984.

————, and Mandelbaum, Michael. *Reagan and Gorbachev.* New York: Vintage Books, 1987.

Valentine, Douglas. *The Hotel Tacloban.* New York: Avon Books, 1984.

Walker, Martin. *The Waking Giant: Gorbachev's Russia.* New York: Pantheon, 1988.

Wallop, Malcolm, and Codevilla, Angelo. *The Arms Control Delusion.* San Francisco: I.C.S. Press, 1987.

Warnke, Paul C. *Star Wars: The Economic Fallout.* Cambridge: Ballinger, 1988.

Wells, Tim. *444 Days: The Hostages Remember.* New York: Harcourt, Brace, Jovanovich, 1984.

White, James E. *Moral Problems.* St. Paul: West Publishing Company, 1988.

————, ed. *Contemporary Moral Problems.* St. Paul: West Publishing Company, 1988.

Wollheim, Richard, ed. *Philosophers on Freud.* New York: Jason Aronson, 1974.

Zuckerman, Lord. *Star Wars in a Nuclear World.* New York: Vintage Books, 1987.

## PERIODICALS

Alperowitz, Gar. "America's Europe Problem." *New Republic*, September 29, 1986, 16.

Andelman, David A. "Struggle Over Western Europe." *Foreign Policy* (Winter 1982–1983):37–51, Vol. 62, No. 4.

Ball, Robert. "Why the Europeans Don't Think Like Us." *Fortune*, August 9, 1982, 38–39.

Brezhnev, Leonid. "The European Conference in Helsinki." *Vital Speeches*, September 1, 1975, 371–79.

————. "The International Situation." *Vital Speeches*, February 15, 1979, 471–5.

————. "American Nuclear Missile Weapons in Western Europe." *Vital Speeches*, November 1, 1979, 33–35.

Brockman, Richard. "Notes While Being Hijacked." *Atlantic*, December 1976, 68–75.

Brummer, Alex. "Thatcher to Take Missile Fears to Washington." *Manchester Guardian Weekly*, October 26, 1986, 1.

Bukovsky, Valdimir. "The Peace Movement and the Soviet Union." *Commentary*, May 1982, 3–20.

Calleo, David P. "NATO's Middle Course." *Foreign Policy* (Winter 1987–1988): 135–47, No. 64.

Carter, Jimmy. "444 Days of Agony." *Time*, October 8, 1982, 47–59.

Chaze, William L. "The 52 Americans Held Hostage." *U.S. News and World Report*, January 16, 1981, 64–7.

Daniels, Robert V. "America's Doubting Allies." *The New Leader*, June 3–17, 1985, 13–4.

Davis, Lynn E. "Lessons of the INF Treaty." *Foreign Affairs* (Spring 1988):720–34, Vol. 66, No. 1.

Derickson, Uli. "I'm No Heroine." *Reader's Digest*, September 1985, 111–19.

Dimsdale, Joe E. "The Coping Behaviors of Nazi Concentration Camp Survivors." *American Journal of Psychiatry* (July 1974):792–97, Vol. 131, No. 7.

Dole, Senator Bob. "What to Do About the Russians." *Policy Review* (Fall 1986): Vol. 16, No. 3.

Drake, Susan. "Why the Allies Hung Back." *Newsweek*, February 4, 1980, 79.

Dudney, Robert S. "NATO's Dilemma: Stopping Russia Without Nuclear Weapons." *U.S. News and World Report*, December 12, 1983, 77.

Ecclestone, Jacob. "Stress: Making Friends of Enemies." *International Journal of Offender Theory and Comparative Criminology* (November 1980): Vol. 46, p. 179.

"Europe and the Bomb." *The Economist*, October 4, 1986, 78.

Evangelista, Matthew A. "The Myth of Hostage Europe." *Nation*, May 7, 1983, 36–8.

Fairhall, David. "Party in Need of a Convincing Salesman." *Manchester Guardian Weekly*, October 5, 1986, 11.

———. "Superpower Arms in Balance." *Manchester Guardian Weekly*, November 16, 1986, 8.

Fenyesi, Charles. "The Hostages: Re-Entry Problems Ahead." *Psychology Today*, August 1980, 9–10.

Gettinger, Stephen. "Hostage Negotiators Bring Them Out Alive." *Police Magazine*, January 1983, 69–75.

Gold, Philip. "Pact and Impact: A Waiting Game." *Insight*, February 22, 1988, 8–18.

Gromyko, Andrei. "The International Situation." *Vital Speeches*, July 15, 1983, 671–5.

Hamburg, Roger. "Soviet Policy in Western Europe." *Current History* (May 1981): 220–25, Vol. 36.

Hillman, Robert G. "The Psychopathology of Being Held Hostage." *American Journal of Psychiatry* (September 1981):1193–97, Vol. 11.

Hough, Jerry F. "Gorbachev Won't Play by Reagan's Rules." *The Washington Post Weekly*, September 8, 1986, 25–6.

Ignatius, David, and Gelter, Michael. "New Rules in the Game with Moscow." *Manchester Guardian Weekly*, December 20, 1987, 19.

Jacobson, Sylvia. "Individual and Group Response to Confinement in a Skyjacked Plane." *American Journal of Orthopsychiatry* (April 1973):459–69, Vol. 43, No. 3.

Jenkins, Brian M. "Hostages and Their Captors—Friends and Lovers." *The Rand Corporation*, October 1975, 1–12.

Keerdoja, Eileen. "Hostage Syndrome." *Newsweek*, May 8, 1978, 101.

Kennan, George F. "The Gorbachev Prospect." *The New York Review of Books*, January 21, 1988, 3-6.

Kimelman, Donald. "Editor Gorbo." *New Republic*, September 7, 1987, 13-14.

"Kinnock in America." *The Economist*, November 22-28, 1986.

Kohut, Andrew. "What Americans Want." *Foreign Policy* (Spring 1988):150-65, No. 70.

Krauthammer, Charles. "The Week Washington Lost Its Head." *New Republic*, January 4, 1988, 18-19.

"Labor and European Defense." *Manchester Guardian Weekly*, December 7, 1986, 11-12.

Lacquer, Walter. "The Specter of Finlandization." *Commentary*, December 1977, 37-41.

———. "Euro-Neutralism." *Commentary*, June 1980, 21-26.

Lang, Daniel. "A Reporter at Large: The Bank Drama." *The New Yorker*, November 25, 1974, 56-60.

Lee, Steven. "The Morality of Nuclear Deterrence: Hostage Holding and Consequences." *Ethics*, April 1985, 267-88.

Matthews, Thomas. "A Psychiatrist's Notes." *Newsweek*, February 16, 1976, 44.

McCarthy, Abigail. "Voices of Their Captors." *Commonweal*, February 15, 1980, 81-2.

Mroz, John. "Gorbachev After Three Years." *New York Times*, March 10, 1988, 29.

Nixon, Richard M. "Dealing With Gorbachev." *New York Times Magazine*, March 3, 1988, 26-30.

"Noises Off." *The Economist*, September 27, 1986, 64.

Noyes, Russell. "Depersonalization in the Face of Life Threatening Dangers: A Description." *Psychiatry* (February 1976): Vol. 31, No. 2.

Nye, Joseph S., Jr. "Farewell to Arms Control?" *Foreign Affairs* (Fall 1986):1-20, Vol. 65, No. 1.

Oates, Joyce Carol. "Intellectual Seduction." *New York Times Magazine*, January 3, 1988, 16-19.

Pick, Hella. "The Spirit of Reykjavik is Dead." *Manchester Guardian Weekly*, November 16, 1986, 13.

Pipes, Richard. "How to Cope with the Soviet Threat: A Long-Term Strategy for the West." *Commentary*, August 1984, 3-18.

Puddington, Arch. "The New Soviet Apologists." *Commentary*, November 1983, 8-19.

Rabinowitz, Dorothy. "The Hostage Mentality." *Commentary*, June 1977, 70-72.

Rachwald, Arthur R. "The Soviet Approach to West Europe." *Current History* (October 1983):309-14, Vol. 38.

Record, Jeffrey, and Rivkia, David B., Jr. "Defending Post-INF Europe." *Foreign Affairs* (Spring 1988):Vol. 66, No. 4, 735-54.

Rosen, Barbara, and Rosen, Barry. "The Destined Hour." *Reader's Digest*, July 1982, 173-191.

Rosenthal, A. M. "Gorbachev's Hidden Agenda." *New York Times*, December 12, 1987, 24.

Rosenthal, Irwin. "Vietnam War Soldiers and the Experience of Normlessness." *Journal of Social Psychology* (1975): Vol. 37, 311-321.

Sancton, Thomas A. "Smoothing the Way." *Time*, November 17, 1980, p. 41.

_____ . "The Spirit of Washington." *New York Times Magazine*, December 21, 1987, 16-21.

Shulman, Marshall D. "The Superpowers: Dance of the Dinosaurs." *Foreign Affairs*, (Winter 1987-1988):494-515, Vol. 66, No. 3.

Simes, Dimitri. "Did the Summit Change Anything?" *New York Times*, October 26, 1986, p. 34.

Smith, Jeffrey. "Missile Deployments Shake European Politics." *Science*, February 1984, 665-67.

_____ . "The Nitty-Gritty of Destroying Missiles." *Manchester Guardian Weekly*, December 13, 1987, 17.

Starr, Richard F. "Soviet Relations with East Europe." *Current History* (April 1978): 145-49, 33.

Steele, Jonathan. "Time to Respond Positively to Gorbachev." *Manchester Guardian Weekly*, August 24, 1986, 11.

"Streetwise Mikhail." *The Economist*, July 26, 1986, 31-2.

Svec, Milan. "Removing Gorbachev's Ego." *Foreign Policy* (Winter 1987-1988): 148-65, Vol. 66, No. 2.

Taylor, Robert. "Hostage and Crisis Negotiation Procedures." *Trial*, March 1983, 47-56.

"The Sentry at the Gate: A Survey of NATO's Central Front." *The Economist*, August 30, 1986, 78-97.

"The 38 Hours: Trial by Terror." *Time*, March 21, 1977, 46-57.

Trewhitt, Henry. "But Will We Still Love Him Tomorrow." *U.S. News and World Report*, December 21, 1987, 20-40.

Vessey, John W. "The Unrelenting Growth of Soviet Military Power." *Vital Speeches*, 456-59.

Wardlaw, Grant. "The Psychologist's Role in Hostage Negotiations." *The Police Chief*, May 1984, 37-43.

Weinberger, Caspar W. "Arms Reduction and Deterrence." *Foreign Affairs* (Spring 1988):700-19, Vol. 66, No. 4.

Yankelovich, Daniel, and Doble, John. "The Public Mood." *Foreign Affairs* (Fall 1984):33-46, Vol. 63, No. 1.

# Index

# About the Author

PHILIP PILEVSKY, president and sole owner of Philips International, has distinguished himself as one of the most active real estate buyers and developers in New York. A recent venture was the phased co-op conversion of Tudor City.

Philip Pilevsky is also a guest lecturer at Columbia University and sits on the advisory board of Columbia's master of science program in real estate development. He has also lectured before the Wharton Club of New York, given a series of six lectures on International Relations at Long Island University, and continues to teach real estate and political science courses at New York University.